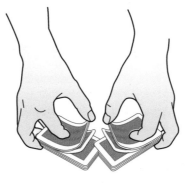

Basic
Bridge

First published in Great Britain in 2003 by
Hamlyn, a division of Octopus Publishing Group Ltd
2–4 Heron Quays, London E14 4JP

Distributed in the United States and Canada by
Sterling Publishing Co., Inc.
387 Park Avenue South
New York, NY 10016-8810

ISBN 0 600 60803 4

A CIP catalogue record for this book is available
from the British Library

Card designs based on Waddingtons
No. 1 Playing Cards.

WADDINGTONS NO. 1 PLAYING CARDS
© 2003 Hasbro International Inc.
Used with kind permission of Hasbro.

Publisher's Note
Throughout this book individual players have been
referred to as 'he'. This is simply for convenience
and in no way reflects an opinion that Bridge is a
male-only game.

Printed and bound in the United Arab Emirates

10 9 8 7 6 5 4 3 2 1

Basic
Bridge

Peter Arnold

CONTENTS

INTRODUCTION

Bridge is a simple game to learn. Yet so many people who would like to play, and who indeed are good players of other card games, are put off. Perhaps they have read a Bridge column in a newspaper and failed to make head or tail of it, or opened a book for beginners in the middle and been baffled.

When I was asked to write an introductory book I jumped at the chance. Most books, it seems to me, are written for people who play already, and those that are aimed at beginners get too technical too quickly. In many books, the niceties of Bridge are being discussed before the learner has an overall grasp of what the whole game is about.

To combat this I have devoted the first part of this book to explaining the mechanics of the game, step by step, without going in to what exactly makes 'good' play. In fact, this section presents a specimen game that includes some examples of bad play, to show what would happen.

Introduction

As soon as you have digested this section, you can start to play. Not well, of course – parts two and three of the book help a little towards that – but once you start, you will soon learn and improve your play. Ideally, the best way to learn is to find four or five friends with whom to practise. Perhaps you might like to buy a couple of copies of this book and pass them round. As you play you can discuss the hands and you will all improve. I learned in this way about 40 years ago with a few colleagues during lunchtimes at the office, but we had the additional advantage that one of us already played. She was prepared to instruct us and, at the same time, be patient while we approached a standard that made the games interesting for her. I hope this book will inspire some readers to find an equally long-lasting pleasure in the game.

There are two points I would like to make about the book. I have used the pronoun 'he' when discussing an individual player, although I know there are as many women players as men. 'He or she' is tedious, to alternate 'he' and 'she' could be confusing and I have never liked the modern practice of calling a single person 'they' – besides, I have used 'they' for the partnership. I hope female readers will forgive me.

I have also used the practice, common in Bridge books, of putting the suit before the rank when referring to a card, and the number before the suit for a bid or contract – ♦ 2, ♠ 3, ♥ 4 refer to the playing cards two of diamonds, three of spades, four of hearts while 2 ♦, 3 ♠, 4 ♥ refer to bids or contracts of two diamonds, three spades and four hearts respectively. The context hardly ever allows confusion, but it is one of those things you should know about the game.

♠
♥
♦
♣

GETTING TO KNOW BRIDGE

1

GETTING TO KNOW BRIDGE

* *

In this first part we start with a basic outline of Bridge, then look at each part of the game in turn, ending with a specimen rubber.

Basic outline

Bridge is a game for four people, two playing as partners against the other two. A standard pack of cards, without jokers, is used. (See also Shuffling, page 14). The pack is dealt so that each player has 13 cards. Like Whist, Hearts or Black Maria, Bridge involves winning tricks. One player leads a card and the other three players follow, the player who leads the highest-value card claiming the trick (the set of four cards) for his side. There are therefore 13 tricks to be won in each deal or hand.

But winning at Bridge is not merely a question of winning more tricks than the other side. Its beauty lies in the *auction*, which takes place between dealing and playing the cards. In the auction, each player evaluates his hand and in turn (clockwise round the table) makes a *call*, which might be a *pass* or a *bid*. In effect a bid states that the player who makes it and his partner undertake to win a certain number of tricks in that deal. Each bid must be higher than the previous bid and when a player feels his hand is not strong enough to justify bidding further he passes. Calling continues until three consecutive passes have been made, when it ends. The last

bid is called the *contract*, and the side making it has contracted to make (win) at least as many tricks as the contract states. Play then begins.

The success or failure of the contracting side to make the number of tricks stated determines the number of points that they or their opponents score. There are certain bonuses or penalties that can be incurred in the scoring but basically that is how Bridge is played: one side contracts to make a certain number of tricks and then attempts to make them, while the other side tries to prevent them. Solo-whist players will already be familiar with the principle. We will look at each of the stages in turn. But to begin at the beginning...

The pack

As stated above, a standard pack of cards, containing 52 cards is used. These 52 are divided into four suits: spades (♠), hearts (♥), diamonds (♦) and clubs (♣). There are 13 cards in each suit. In Bridge the four suits are not of equal value.

Spades and hearts are called the *major suits* (see Figure 1) and diamonds and clubs the *minor suits* (see Figure 2).

The ranking of the suits is for the purposes of bidding and scoring. It does not mean that in playing the cards all spades are worth more than any heart, diamond or club. It means, as we shall see later, that as far as bidding goes, a bid to make seven tricks with diamonds

THE CARDS

Suits rank in the following order:

HIGHEST   LOWEST

| Spades | Hearts | Diamonds | Clubs |
| 1st | 2nd | 3rd | 4th |

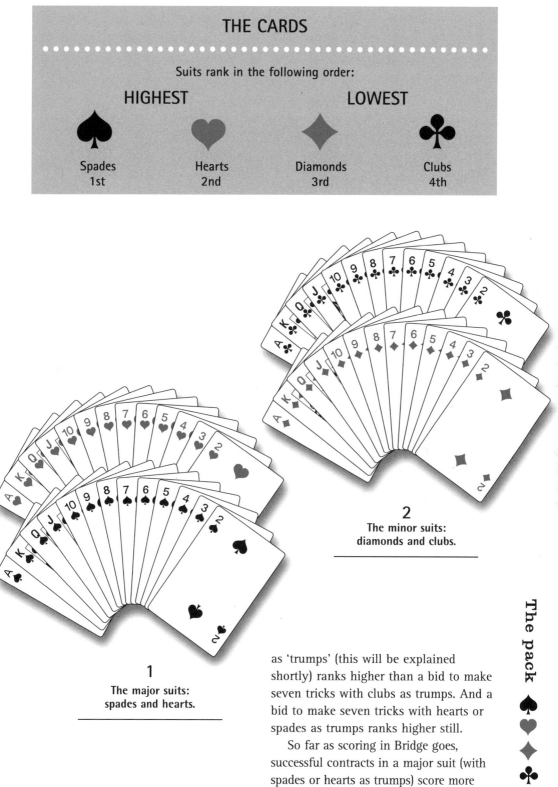

1
The major suits:
spades and hearts.

2
The minor suits:
diamonds and clubs.

as 'trumps' (this will be explained shortly) ranks higher than a bid to make seven tricks with clubs as trumps. And a bid to make seven tricks with hearts or spades as trumps ranks higher still.

So far as scoring in Bridge goes, successful contracts in a major suit (with spades or hearts as trumps) score more points than those in a minor suit (diamonds or clubs).

The values of the cards from highest to lowest within suits are as follows: A, K, Q, J, 10, 9, 8, 7, 6, 5, 4, 3, 2.

If dealt four of the five honour cards (see box below) in one suit, or all four Aces, you can score bonus points, as we will see later.

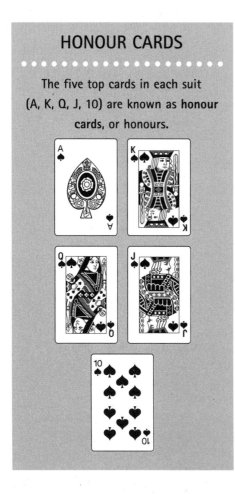

HONOUR CARDS

● ●

The five top cards in each suit (A, K, Q, J, 10) are known as **honour cards**, or **honours**.

Seating

Bridge has inspired a huge literature, much more than any other card game, and in it over the years, the convention has grown that the four players are described by the points of the compass: North, South, East and West. Partners sit opposite each other, North/South being one partnership and East/West the other. They occupy the positions shown in Figure 3.

Choosing partners

Some partnerships in games of Bridge are pre-arranged: for example, four friends meeting for a game might decide that the strongest player should partner the weakest against the other two players.

Otherwise, the conventional way of choosing partners is to draw for it. Before the players take their seats, one shuffles a pack of cards and spreads it face down on the table. Each player then draws a card from the pack, and the two who choose the highest cards play against the other two. The cards rank Ace high down to 2 and the suit matters only if two or more cards of the same rank are drawn. For example, if the four cards drawn are those shown in Figure 4, the drawers of ♣ K and ♥ 6 would be partners, as the ♥ 6 would rank above the ♦ 6, because hearts rank higher than diamonds.

The drawers of the two highest cards also have the choice of seats.

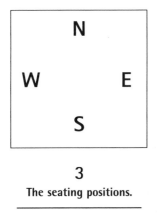

3
The seating positions.

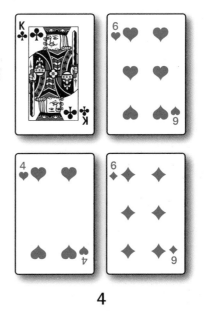

4
The draw.

Remember, that partners sit opposite each other at the table. The player who drew the highest card deals first.

The partnerships are kept until the end of the rubber, which consists of the best of three 'games', either by two games to nil or two games to one (see Winning a Rubber, page 28).

SHUFFLING AND DEALING

	North	East	South	West
Hands 1, 5, 9 and so on	Shuffles pack 2 for next hand	Cuts pack 1 before hand	Deals pack 1	(Has already shuffled pack 1)
Hands 2, 6 and so on	(Has already shuffled pack 2)	Shuffles pack 1 for next hand	Cuts pack 2 before hand	Deals pack 2
Hands 3, 7 and so on	Deals pack 1	(Has already shuffled pack 1)	Shuffles pack 2 for next hand	Cuts pack 1 before hand
Hands 4, 8 and so on	Cuts pack 2 before hand	Deals pack 2	(Has already shuffled pack 2)	Shuffles pack 1 for next hand

Choosing partners ♠ ♥ ♦ ♣

Shuffling

It is usual in Bridge to play with two packs of cards. This saves considerable time shuffling between deals. Suppose South is to deal. The cards have been shuffled by the player on his left, West, who is of course an opponent. West places the shuffled pack in front of his partner, East, who cuts it into two piles by taking a pile from the top and placing it on the table. The dealer then completes the cut by placing the original bottom half of the pack on top and proceeds to deal. While he is dealing, North is shuffling the other pack of cards, with which West will deal the second hand. When he has done this he places the cards to his right.

When the cards are collected up after each deal, they are in the form of the separate tricks that have been played and are thus in groups of four cards, many of which will be groups of the same suit. Therefore the cards need to be shuffled thoroughly before they are used for the next hand.

Shuffling methods

There are two main methods of shuffling. The more popular is the hand-over-hand shuffle, in which the pack is held face down on the fingers of the left hand (assuming you are right-handed). The right hand takes most of the cards from the bottom of the pack (the left thumb holds a few back) and drops

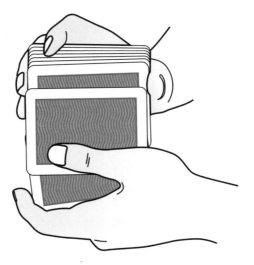

The normal hand-over-hand.

them in little packets (again helped by the left thumb) on to the top of the packet retained in the left hand. This must be done several times to ensure a random distribution of cards in the pack.

The other method is the riffle, where the pack is divided into two, the halves being placed on the table face down close to each other. Opposite corners of the two halves are bent upwards, the two halves pushed together so that the corners overlap and the cards released gradually and simultaneously so that they interlock. It has been proven that you need to do this shuffle seven times to produce a completely random deck.

I prefer the hand-over-hand method as I do not like bending cards. In both cases the object is to mix up the cards thoroughly so that they are in as random an order as possible.

Dealing

When the pack has been shuffled and cut, the dealer distributes the cards one at a time to each player in a clockwise direction, beginning with the player on his left. If a card is exposed during the deal, the cards must be collected up, reshuffled, cut and dealt again.

When the hand has been played, the deal passes to the left, clockwise round the table (see table, page 13). If all the players pass rather than bid on a hand, the current dealer does not redeal; the deal passes to the player on the left.

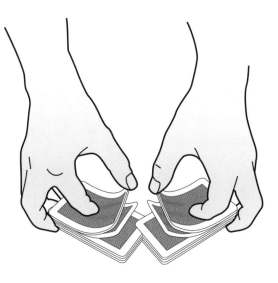

The riffle.

Sorting

Players should not touch the cards as they are being dealt, and should wait until the dealer has finished before picking up their hands and sorting them into an order that tells them at a glance the number of cards held in each suit.

The easiest way to sort your hand so that you can see exactly what you have, making it less likely that you make a mistake in the play, is to sort the cards into alternate black and red suits, making a fan with the spades on the left followed successively by hearts, clubs and diamonds. This is not quite in their order of value, which would entail the clubs and diamonds changing places. But this would mean the hearts and diamonds would form a red block and make it less easy to see where one suit ends and the other starts. Within each suit, the cards are most conveniently ranged highest on the left and lowest on the right. Under this arrangement your hand might look like either of those in Figure 5.

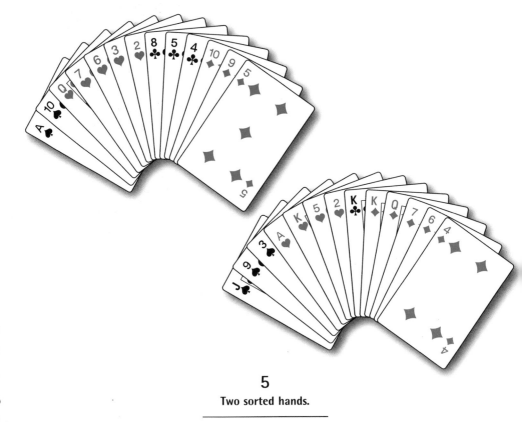

5

Two sorted hands.

♠ ♥ ♦ ♣ Getting to know Bridge

Giving the game away

Some books advocate this method of sorting cards and for convenience it will be the one used in illustrating hands in this book. However, it does have a drawback in that if you follow it without variation it allows opponents to make deductions about your hand from the cards you play. For example, suppose you held the bottom hand illustrated in Figure 5 and decided to lead your Ace of hearts. By noting that it was the fourth card in your hand, your opponents could infer immediately that you held three spades. This is very valuable information. Similarly, if a spade were led and you played the Jack, taking it from the left-hand end of your fan, opponents could deduce that you do not hold the Ace, King or Queen.

If an opponent led the Ace of clubs and you were forced to follow with the King, opponents could infer that you held seven cards in the major suits and possibly five in diamonds. So although the method illustrated is the most convenient way to sort a hand, it might be as well not to use it in every deal, but sometimes to change the order of the suits or range the cards in rank from low to high, or even not to rank some suits in order at all.

Tricks and trumps

As stated in the Basic Outline (see page 10), there are two main parts to Bridge: the auction (bidding) that determines which side is to attempt to make a certain number of tricks, and the play. Before discussing the bidding, which follows the cards being dealt, we must understand what is meant by tricks and trumps, so we must take a quick look at the play before we can understand how the bidding works.

During the play, each player in turn clockwise round the table will lay down a card. These four cards constitute a *trick*. Since during the deal each player will play 13 cards to the table, there are 13 tricks in a hand. Each trick is won by the best card laid. The first card played in the first trick of each hand is called the *lead*, and the first lead is made by the player to the left of the *declarer*, who is determined by the

TRUMP SUITS

• •

The word 'trump' is believed to derive from the word 'triumph'. A card in the trump suit outranks, or triumphs over cards from any of the other suits.

bidding, as we shall see shortly. Subsequently each lead is made by the winner of the previous trick.

With one exception, the card that wins the trick is the highest card in the suit of the lead card. When the lead has been made, all other players must *follow suit* – play a card of the same suit as that led if they have any. The simplest trick would be that shown in Figure 6. West led the ♦ 10 and East won the trick with the ♦ A.

If a player does not have a card of the suit led, he may *discard* by playing any card he wishes. This might lead to a trick like that in Figure 7. As winner of the previous trick, East led the ♦ K. South and North followed suit, but West held no more diamonds and discarded the ♣ 2. East again won the trick. In each of these cases, the highest card in the suit led won the trick.

Using trumps

However, there is an exception when the highest card does not necessarily win the trick. Most hands are played with one of the suits as *trumps*. The side winning the contract agrees to make a certain number of tricks with a trump suit of their choice. How trumps are chosen is explained in the bidding, on page 19. A card of the trump suit outranks any card of the other three suits, which are called *side suits*.

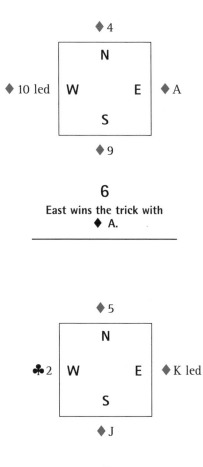

♦ 4

N

♦ 10 led | W   E | ♦ A

S

♦ 9

6

East wins the trick with ♦ A.

♦ 5

N

♣ 2 | W   E | ♦ K led

S

♦ J

7

West discards.

In Figure 8, hearts have been chosen as trumps. East, having won the previous trick with ♦ K, now leads the ♦ 2. South plays the ♦ Q with little hope of winning the trick, although this is the highest diamond left to be played. He knows West is *void* in diamonds – that is, he doesn't possess a diamond. West trumps with the ♥ 2 and wins the trick when North is forced to follow suit to the diamond lead. Another word for trumping is *ruffing*. In the example in Figure 8, had North also been void in diamonds, he might have *overruffed* with any heart higher than West's ♥ 2, and won the trick.

Now that we know how tricks are won, and the value of the trump suit in winning them, we can look more closely at how the bidding is conducted.

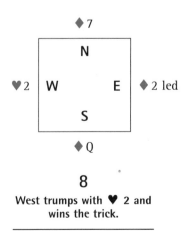

8
West trumps with ♥ 2 and wins the trick.

Outline of bidding

The bidding (otherwise known as the auction) takes place after the cards are dealt and before the play. The object of the players on each side is to reach a *contract* that suits their combined hands. They cannot compare hands with each other of course, so a player who makes an opening bid is promising that he and his partner will make (win) a certain number of tricks without knowing what sort of hand his partner holds. His partner's bid in response will pass some information back and subsequent bids by partners and opponents will enable each player to draw inferences about the other players' hands.

In making a bid, the player states which suit will be trumps, or if the hand will be played without trumps. In effect the partners are conducting a dialogue, while at the same time listening to their opponents' dialogue.

When making a bid, a player states the number of tricks above six his side proposes to make (clearly, if the side makes more than six tricks they have made the majority of tricks, there being thirteen in a deal). Therefore, a player who bids 'four spades' is contracting to make ten tricks (six plus four), with spades as trumps.

Calling the bid

The players *call* in turn, starting with the dealer. It is not obligatory to bid. A player with a poor hand might *pass*, which is usually expressed either by saying 'pass' (more popular in the USA) or 'no bid' (popular in the UK). A player who passes may subsequently bid when his turn to call comes round again. Each bid must *overbid* the previous bid.

As stated, the suits rank: spades (highest), hearts, diamonds, clubs. The smallest bid that can be made, therefore, is 'one club', which is a promise to make seven tricks with clubs as the trump suit. The next smallest bids are 'one diamond', 'one heart' and 'one spade'. These are called bids at the One level.

No-trumps

There is another type of bid: one of 'no-trumps'. This is a contract to make the majority of tricks without a trump suit. Bids of 'no-trumps' rank above those of any suit, so the call higher than 'one spade' is 'one no-trump'. To overbid a call of 'one no-trump', a subsequent bidder must bid at least 'two clubs' (called a bid at the 'Two level'), a contract to make eight tricks with clubs as trumps.

Double and redouble

Apart from passing or bidding, there are two other calls a player might make. These are 'Double', in which a player confident of beating an opponent's proposed contract can (roughly) double the number of points at stake for the contract (see Scoring, pages 25–28), and 'Redouble', in which a player whose side has been doubled, but who is nevertheless confident of making the contract, can increase the points at stake further to roughly four times the points that would normally be scored for the contract. We will go into this in more detail later.

Bidding ends when three players have passed consecutively, or when the bidding reaches seven no-trumps redoubled, which is the highest bid possible in Bridge.

Putting it all into practice

For an example of a straightforward auction, consider the hands in Figure 9 opposite. South is the dealer and makes the first call. He has a less than average hand, and will probably pass. It is West's turn to bid and his hand, with its strong spade suit and Ace of clubs, is worth an exploratory bid of 'one spade'. This makes West the *opening bidder* and his bid is the *opening bid*. His bid tells his partner that he has a good hand with spades as his strongest suit.

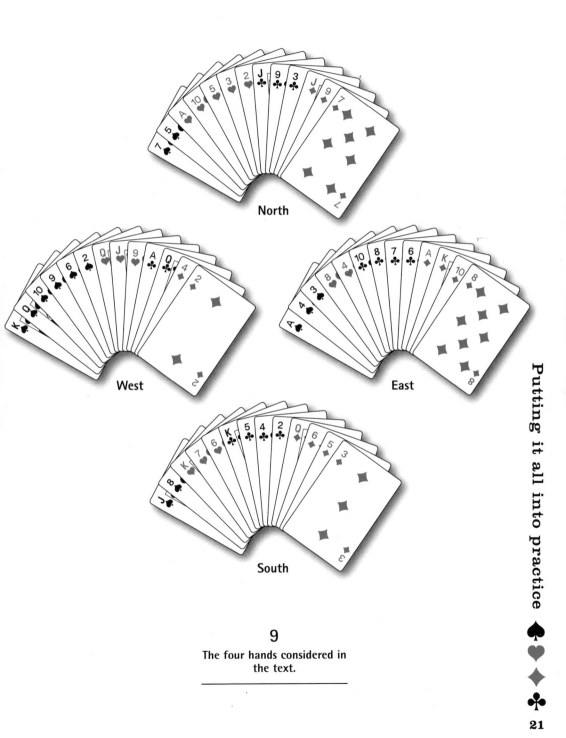

North

West

East

South

9

The four hands considered in
the text.

THE BIDDING

• •

Player	Bid
South	Pass
West	One spade
North	Pass
East	Two diamonds
South	Pass
West	Two spades
North	Pass
East	Four spades
South	Pass
West	Pass
North	Pass

North will probably feel unable to compete, and will pass, and East, holding the Ace of spades, a strong suit of diamonds and the possibility of making a trick with a small trump in the second round of hearts, decides to bid 'two diamonds'. East is called the *responder* but it is not necessary to learn these terms in order to play – it merely helps if you intend to read Bridge columns or books.

East is not competing against his partner for the contract but telling his partner that he is happy to hear his bid of spades and that he himself has a strong suit of diamonds and that his

side have the balance of strength. South will again pass and West might now inform his partner that spades is his only strong suit by bidding 'two spades' (not necessarily the best bid). East must now decide whether his support for his partner in spades is strong enough to bid 'four spades'. Let us say he does. The other players will probably pass, thus ending the auction, and play will begin with East/West having contracted to make ten tricks with spades as trumps and West the declarer.

Don't worry if you can't understand why East bid 'two diamonds' and then 'four spades'. Later in the book it will become clearer. Suffice to say here that East bid four spades because making a contract of four spades earns enough points for a *game*, as we will shortly see in the section entitled Scoring (see pages 25–28).

Bridge notation

Now that we have discussed a deal, and the possible bidding that might result from it, it is worth setting it out in Bridge notation. To save a lot of space in the descriptions of both Bridge hands and the bidding, books and newspaper columns have developed a form of notation which is in general use.

If the deal in Figure 9, with the subsequent bidding as described above, was set out in a newspaper Bridge column, it would probably appear as shown in Figure 10.

The contract

When the bidding has been completed, the side that made the last bid has 'bought' the contract. In the deal already discussed and outlined in Figure 10, East/West have ended in a contract of four spades, which means that with spades as the trump suit, East/West must make at least ten of the thirteen tricks to land the contract and score points. Should they eventually win nine or fewer, they fail, and North/South score points as specified by the scoring rules (see Scoring, pages 25–28).

The player on the contracting side who *first* bid the suit of the contract is called the *declarer*. Note that in the example in Figure 10 West is the declarer, as the first to mention spades, not East who made the final bid of 4 ♠.

The play

The player on the declarer's left is the first to play a card to the table, laying the first card of the first trick. This is called the *opening lead*. The player can play any card he likes. In the example we are following, it is North who lays the first card.

After the opening lead, the declarer's partner (in this case East) places all of the cards in his hand face up on the table. The trump suit is laid to his right (declarer's left as he looks at it). Figure 11 (overleaf) shows how in our example East would lay down his hand on the table. This hand is referred to as the *dummy*.

```
                  ♠ 7 5
                  ♥ A 10 5 3 2
                  ♦ J 9 7
                  ♣ J 9 3
♠ K Q 10 9 6 2         N           ♠ A 4 3
♥ Q J 9                            ♥ 8 4
♦ 4 2          W         E         ♦ A K 10 8
♣ A Q                              ♣ 10 8 7 6
                      S
                  ♠ J 8
                  ♥ K 7 6
                  ♦ Q 6 5 3
                  ♣ K 5 4 2
```

South	West	North	East
No	1 ♠	No	2 ♦
No	2 ♠	No	4 ♠
No	No	No	

10

The hands in Figure 9, and the accompanying bidding as it would usually be set out.

The holder of the dummy, East, takes no further part in the deal, and cannot offer advice to the declarer. The declarer plays his side's cards on his own, both his own hand and the dummy. The two players comprising the other side, who are attempting to prevent the contract being made, are called the *defenders*.

23

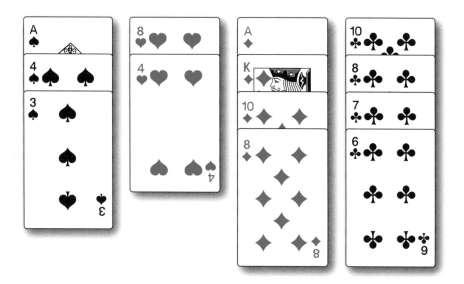

11

How the dummy is laid out.

After the opening lead, the play in the first trick continues in a clockwise fashion round the table. Usually the cards are played roughly one on top of another, as in Figure 12. When each player has played a card, the best card in the trick wins it (in this case the ♥ A with which North led).

The winner of a trick leads the next one, and so on until all 13 tricks have been played.

Finshing a hand

One player on each side collects all the tricks for his own side. They are stacked

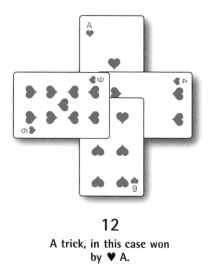

12

A trick, in this case won by ♥ A.

in neat overlapping piles face down so that during play it is clear at a glance how many tricks each side has won. Figure 13 shows a neat pile of six tricks.

At the end of the hand, each side counts its tricks and the points are allocated. Ideally all four players keep both scores, and all four score sheets should tally. The reason for this is to allow each player to know the score at a glance at all stages of the game, since the state of the score might affect how one bids. However, when learning the game, or playing friendly games with family or neighbours, it is usually sufficient for only one score sheet to be kept. In these cases players can ask the state of the game at any time.

When the hand has been played, the next hand is dealt by the player to the left of the previous dealer.

The scoring

It might seem strange to have described each stage of the game but to have left the important question of scoring as late as this. The reason is that to beginners the scoring looks difficult and off-putting. In fact, the important parts soon become almost automatic. If something really remarkable occurs, such as a side going down by five tricks on a vulnerable contract of six no-trumps doubled and redoubled, then you can look up the appropriate penalty. So don't bother to try to learn the scores for every eventuality. After all, a man setting out to learn how to play golf, for example, does not need to be able to recite the rules of the Royal and Ancient Golf Club or know the penalty for carrying two extra clubs in his bag before he starts to play.

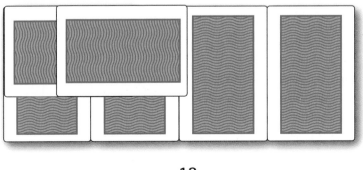

13
Six tricks stacked in
overlapping piles.

♠
♥
♦
♣

SCORES BELOW THE LINE

	No-trumps	Major suit tricks	Minor suit tricks
		(spades or hearts)	(diamonds or clubs)
First trick over six	40	30	20
Subsequent tricks	30	30	20

A full scoring table for quick reference appears near the back of this book (see pages 152–153), but here we will look at the details of how the scoring works. A Bridge score sheet has two columns, one headed 'We' and the other 'They'. A heavy line is drawn across the middle of the sheet and some scores are entered *above the line* and others *below the line*. Figure 14 shows a blank score sheet. To win at Bridge, you must win what is known as a *rubber*. A rubber consists of a set of two or three *games*. How do you win games?

The value of tricks

First of all, you must know the values of the tricks that you have won, and how these values vary according to whether the contract is in no-trumps or in a suit. In no-trumps, the first trick after six counts 40 points, and subsequent tricks 30 points each. In the major suits (spades and hearts), each trick above six counts 30 points. In the minor suits (diamonds and clubs), each trick above six counts for 20 points.

We	They

14

A Bridge score sheet.

Above or below the line?

All points made for making contracts are scored below the line. Other points scored (such as by making *overtricks* – more tricks than you contracted for – or by defeating the opponents' contract) are scored above the line. Above-the-line points contribute to the settlement at the end, and help decide who pays how much and to whom, but for the purposes of winning games and rubbers, they do not count. Only points below the line count in games and rubbers.

Winning a 'game'

To win a 'game', you need to score 100 points below the line. It will be seen from the figures above that making a contract of three no-trumps (3NT) will score 100 points (40 + 30 + 30). This is therefore known as a *game contract*. Similarly, winning a contract of 4 ♠ or 4 ♥ will score 120 points (30 + 30 + 30 + 30). These are also game contracts. To make a game contract in the minor suits, you will have to make 5 ♦ or 5 ♣ (20 + 20 + 20 + 20 + 20 = 100 points).

Therefore, a side that takes the bidding as high as 3NT, 4 ♠, 4 ♥, 5 ♦ or 5 ♣ is said to be *bidding to game*. Clearly it is more difficult to score a game in one hand with diamonds or clubs as trumps, when you must make 11 of the 13 tricks, than it is with spades or hearts as trumps. In no-trumps you need make only 9 of the 13 tricks to score game.

Part-scores

If a side holds only a slight balance of power in the cards dealt, the bidding might not reach high enough for a side to score game. For example, the bidding might end at 2 ♦. If the side contracting to make 2 ♦ succeeds they will score 40 points below the line. This is a *part-score*. It is not enough for game, but it means that on a subsequent hand the side needs only 60 more points for game; making 2NT, 2 ♠ or 2 ♥ enough. If before those 60 points are made, the opponents win a contract of, say, 3NT and reach the 100 points, they will win the game. The 40 points scored for the part-score would count in the final settlement, but not towards the next game and 40 points is hardly significant in Bridge.

It is more valuable, then, to make a game score than a part-score, and while part-scores can turn out to be valuable, it is worth taking a risk to go for game.

When we were discussing bidding (see pages 21–22) in relation to the hands in Figure 10, we pointed out that East bid 4 ♠. This is because 4 ♠ was a game contract. If East had bid 3 ♠ and made 4 ♠ (ten tricks), as East/West should with those hands, it would be disappointing because this would not score game.

If a side bids a part-score, 2 ♦ or 3 ♠, and then makes more tricks, the extra tricks are scored, but above the line. Only the tricks promised in the contract are scored below the line.

Slams

There is a third type of contract as well as part-score and game and this is the *slam*. There are two slams – the *small slam*, which involves contracting and winning 12 tricks, and the *grand slam*, which requires all 13 tricks to be made. The score per trick remains the same but slams carry bonuses of 500 (not vulnerable) and 750 (vulnerable) for a small slam, and 1,000 (not vulnerable) and 1,500 (vulnerable) for a grand slam, all usually scored above the line. Vulnerability is a subject we will get to shortly, but after a few words about winning a rubber, we can summarize what we have learned of the scoring so far by means of a score sheet of a sample rubber (see Figure 15 – the figures in brackets are to allow us to explain which deal each score is for).

Winning a rubber

As we have already said, a rubber consists of three games, a game being a hand (or combination of hands if you only achieve part-scores) where 100 or more points are scored by one of the teams. You can, of course, win a rubber in just two hands if you score at least 100 points in each – there is no point in playing for the third game as whoever wins it, you will still win with the two games you already have. Most rubbers take much longer than this, however. If you win the rubber, you receive bonus points to add to your score (see page 31).

We	They
500 (5)	
500 (3)	20 (2)
	130 (1)
180 (3)	60 (2)
60 (4)	
120 (5)	
1,360	210

15

A score sheet of a completed rubber.

Scoring a sample rubber

Deal 1 The opposition has started well. They bid 3NT and actually made 10 tricks. This gives them a score of 130, which can be written below the line. Strictly speaking, the overtrick should be

Getting to know Bridge

entered above the line (100 below and 30 above), but since they have scored game it is not necessary to divide the score and it is usual in this case to write the whole figure below the line. A line is drawn below the score to indicate that a game has been won and further scores below the line are for the next game.

Deal 2 Your opponents bid 3 ♦ but again made ten tricks. This time the opponents score 60 points below the line for making the contract and score 20 points above the line as a bonus for the overtrick. They need now to score only 40 points below the line (that is, 1NT) to win the second game and the rubber. Things are not looking too good for you.

Deal 3 Excellent news – you receive a powerhouse of a hand, bid 6 ♥, a small slam, and make it by taking exactly 12 tricks. You score 180 points, entered below the line, and score 500 points for making a small slam, which is entered above the line. A second line is drawn below this score to indicate the end of a game. The 60 points your opponents hold as a part-score are now worthless so far as winning the next game is concerned. With both sides having one game, the winner of the next game wins the rubber.

Deal 4 Again the bidding stops short of game at 2 ♥. You are the declarer and make your contract without overtricks and score 60 points below the line.

Deal 5 You bid and make 4 ♠, so score 120 below the line, which gives you the game. You have also won the rubber, and for winning it in three games (2–1) you score a bonus of 500 points, which goes above the line.

The rubber is over and the scores are added up and the totals written at the foot of the score sheet. You have won a rubber that included a small slam, and have 1,360 points, while your opponents have 210, a difference of 1,150.

Vulnerability and penalties

The example score sheet in Figure 15, explained above, did not include any examples of penalties, which are points scored by the opponents when a side fails to make its contract. This is because the penalties differ according to whether a side is *vulnerable* or *not vulnerable*.

A vulnerable side is one that has already won a game. Thus, after the first game, the side that wins it becomes vulnerable, while the other side remains not vulnerable. If each side wins a game, both sides are then vulnerable for the deciding game.

Penalties are higher for a side that is vulnerable. A side that is not vulnerable and fails to make its contract is penalized 50 points for each trick by

PENALTIES

	Non-vulnerable	Vulnerable
Failure to win a contract	50 points per trick short of winning	100 points per trick short of winning
Failure to win a doubled contract	100 points for 1 trick short	200 points for 1 trick short
	300 points for 2 tricks short	500 points for 2 tricks short
	500 points for 3 tricks short	800 points for 3 tricks short
	800 points for 4 tricks short	1,100 points for 4 tricks short
	1,100 points for 5 tricks short	1,400 points for 5 tricks short
	+ 300 points per trick thereafter	+ 300 points per trick thereafter
Failure to win a redoubled contract	200 points for 1 trick short	400 points for 1 trick short
	600 points for 2 tricks short	1,000 points for 2 tricks short
	1,000 points for 3 tricks short	1,600 points for 3 tricks short
	1,600 points for 4 tricks short	2,200 points for 4 tricks short
	2,200 points for 5 tricks short	2,800 points for 5 tricks short
	+ 600 points per trick thereafter	+ 600 points per trick thereafter

♠
♥
♦
♣

Getting to know Bridge

which it falls short. However, if the side is vulnerable, failure costs 100 points per trick. These penalties are written above the line on the score sheet.

When the contract has been *doubled* (see page 20), the penalties are more severe than merely doubling the points conceded. A non-vulnerable side is penalized 100 points for being one trick short when doubled, 300 for two short, 500 for three short, 800 for four short, 1,100 for five short, and 300 per trick thereafter. A vulnerable side is penalized 200 points for one trick short, 500 for two short, 800 for three short, 1,100 for four short and 1,400 for five short, again with 300 per trick thereafter.

When the contract has been *redoubled*, the penalties are twice those that apply to a doubled contract.

Doubled and redoubled contracts that are made

When a contract is doubled or redoubled and won the score for the hand is multiplied by two or four, respectively. For example, a successful contract of 4 ♠ is worth 120 points, thus it is worth 240 points doubled and 480 points redoubled. These scores can be written below the line. It is therefore possible for a side to be *doubled into game*. For example, suppose a side contracts to make 2 ♥, which if successful would produce a part-score of 60. If their opponents doubled them and they made the contract they would score 120 and win the game.

When a doubled or redoubled contract is made with overtricks, the overtricks are scored at standard rates, whatever the suit. If not vulnerable, each overtrick is worth 100 above the line if doubled, 200 if redoubled. If vulnerable, each overtrick is worth 200 doubled and 400 redoubled.

In addition to all the scores listed above, there is a 50-point bonus above the line for making a doubled contract and 100 points if redoubled. Bridge players call these points a bonus for the 'insult'.

Bonuses for winning the rubber

As mentioned earlier, there is a bonus for winning the rubber. This is 700 points if the rubber is won two games to nil, 500 points if it is won two games to one. If a rubber cannot be finished, there is a bonus of 300 points for a side that is a game ahead, and 100 points for a part-score in an unfinished game.

Bonuses for honour cards

Aces, Kings, Queens, Jacks and 10s are called honour cards. If one player, whether playing or defending, holds four honours in the trump suit he is awarded a bonus of 100 points above the line, or 150 points for all five honours. A player can also score a bonus of 150 points for holding all four Aces in a no-trump contract, whether playing or defending. These points can be claimed at any time, but it is best if they are claimed after the hand has been completed. Many Bridge players would

♠
♥
♦
♣

like to see the end of these bonuses, believing that sides shouldn't get points just for the luck of being dealt certain cards, and some agree to ignore it.

Penalties and bonuses in play

You can begin to play Bridge without knowing the exact values of all these penalties and bonuses which, while you are at the learning stages (and beyond), you can look up as you go along. But you should get a feel of the principles of the scoring. For example, if you read the Bridge columns in newspapers or magazines you will see the expert writers referring to *sacrifice* bids. What this means is that if your opponents look certain to have the cards to make 4 ♥, which would give them game and rubber, while you hold a strong spade suit, it might be worth you making a 'sacrifice' bid of 4 ♠, even though you do not expect to make the contract. A penalty of 300 points for being two short doubled might be better than letting your opponents make game.

Although you do not need to have all the figures in your head while learning the game, you should know the principles, so that when you read the Bridge columns you at least know what they're talking about.

Specimen rubber

Between the basic outline of Bridge and a fuller consideration of the bidding and the play, here we run through a specimen

rubber to recap what we have learned and put it all into practice. This will provide a sort of revision of what has been covered so far. The description of the rubber can be followed from the page, but you may find it more helpful if you deal a pack of cards into the hands discussed, and play the tricks as the games unfold on the pages.

Starting the game

Four players, A, B, C and D, get together for a rubber of Bridge. From a pack spread out on the table, each draws a card: A draws ♦ 7, B draws ♣ Q, C draws ♦ 2 and D draws ♠ 9. As the drawers of the two highest cards, B and D are partners and will play against players A and C.

The ♣ Q drawn by B gives him the choice of seat he would like at the table. Let us say he chooses the South seat. D will sit North and A and C will sit East and West. We will now, as is customary in Bridge literature, refer to the players by using the terms of North, South, East and West.

The first hand

South, as the drawer of the highest card, is the dealer in the first game. He is entitled to choose which of the two packs of cards being used he will deal. (It makes no difference, of course, but this is the convention which earlier players decided upon to prevent the million-to-one chance of a dispute.)

SUMMARY OF BONUSES

Winning a doubled contract	Double the scores for the hand + 50 points above the line on the score card
Winning a redoubled contract	Multiply the hand score by 4 + 100 points above the line on the score card
Overtricks in a doubled contract	Non-vulnerable: 100 points above the line on the score card Vulnerable: 200 points above the line on the score card
Overtricks in a redoubled contract	Non-vulnerable: 200 points above the line on the score card Vulnerable: 400 points above the line on the score card
Winning a rubber	700 points if won 2–0 500 points if won 2–1
If a rubber cannot be finished	300 points for the side in the lead 100 points for a part-score in a game
Honour cards (A, K, Q, J, 10)	100 points for 4 honour cards in the trump suit 150 points for 5 honour cards in the trump suit 150 points for all 4 Aces in a no-trump contract

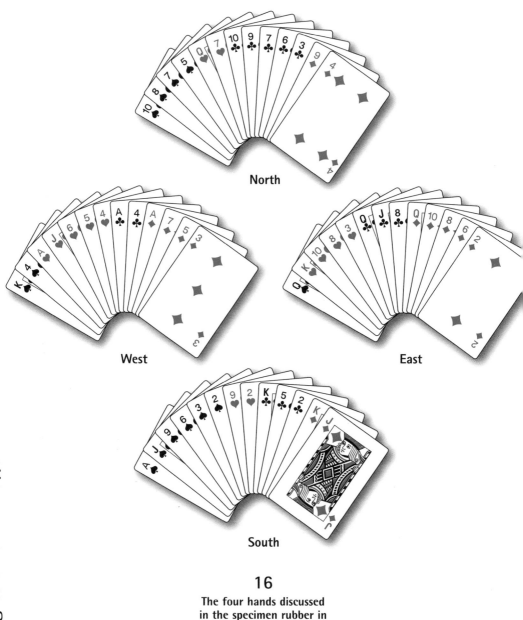

North

West

East

South

16
The four hands discussed
in the specimen rubber in
the text.

So West will shuffle this pack of cards and pass them to East, who will cut the pack into two piles. South will make the pack whole again, and is ready to deal. Each player's has his score sheet and pencil to his right.

While South is dealing, North is shuffling the second pack ready for West to deal the next hand. The hands dealt by South are shown in Figure 16.

When the deal is finished (never start to pick up your cards while the deal is in progress), all players pick up their cards and sort them into their suits.

Bidding

The dealer (South) opens the bidding, and decides, with a six-card spade suit and two other Kings, to open with 1 ♠. West, with three Aces, a reasonable heart suit and (on the assumption that South holds the ♠ A) a probable winner with his own ♠ K, decides to *overcall* with 2 ♥. North, although he has four spades to support his partner if South played in a spade contract, has a poor hand and decides to pass. East, with strong support for his partner's heart suit and 'bits and pieces' in the minor suits, calls 4 ♥, a game contract. He wonders about the chances of a slam, but in view of the fact that South must have a good hand to open the bidding he decides not to encourage his partner too much. His partner will be happy to let the bidding end at 4 ♥, which he does. The hands and bidding, as they would usually appear in Bridge literature, are shown in Figure 17.

Why players make certain bids, and what players can deduce from each others' bids, will be discussed in the next chapter.

Play begins

West, the first player to nominate hearts as the trump suit, becomes the declarer. The player to his left, North, makes the opening lead. The tricks are as follows:

```
                    ♠ 10 8 7 5
                    ♥ Q 7
                    ♦ 9 4
                    ♣ 10 9 7 6 3
   ♠ K 4              N            ♠ Q
   ♥ A J 6 5 4                     ♥ K 10 8 3
   ♦ A 7 5 3      W       E        ♦ Q 10 8 6 2
   ♣ A 4                           ♣ Q J 8
                    S
                    ♠ A J 9 6 3 2
                    ♥ 9 2
                    ♦ K J
                    ♣ K 5 2
```

South	West	North	East
1 ♠	2 ♥	No	4 ♥
No	No	No	

17

The four hands in Figure 16, plus the bidding, in the most convenient form.

Trick 1: North, knowing that he and his partner probably hold at least nine spades, with every chance that his partner holds the Ace, leads ♠ 5. Before another card is played, East lays his cards on the table, in the manner of Figure 11, with the trump suit, hearts, on his right. East takes no further part in the hand. West, as the declarer, now plays the dummy hand, and in trick 1 has no alternative but to play the ♠ Q. South lays ♠ A and West ♠ 4, which, as he had anticipated, leaves the ♠ K in his own hand as the master spade. Tricks: 1–0 to N/S.

Trick 2: South, having won the first trick, leads ♣ 2, hoping that if his partner does not hold ♣ A, West will play it and South's ♣ K becomes good. However, West, who now holds the masters in all four suits, is in no hurry to step in and plays the ♣ 4. North plays ♣ 10 and the declarer wins with the dummy's ♣ Q. Tricks: 1–1.

Trick 3: West, who can see eight more tricks coming his way for certain, decides to test the trumps. He leads ♥ 3 from the dummy. South plays ♥ 2, West plays ♥ A, and North plays ♥ 7. Tricks: 2–1 to E/W.

Trick 4: West decides to play as if North holds ♥ Q and now leads ♥ 4 from his hand. The only outstanding hearts are ♥ Q and ♥ 9, and declarer intends to play ♥ 10 from the dummy if North plays ♥ 9. This will lose a trick if South holds ♥ Q, but playing ♥ K would lose the trick if North held ♥ Q. In the event, North plays ♥ Q and the declarer plays ♥ K from the dummy. South has to play ♥ 9. The declarer's decision turned out well, and he has now cleared all the trumps. Tricks: 3–1 E/W.

Trick 5: The declarer leads ♦ 10 from the dummy. South covers with ♦ J, the declarer uses his ♦ A, and North follows with ♦ 4. Tricks: 4–1 E/W.

Trick 6: The declarer leads ♦ 3 intending to cover any card played by North (unless it is ♦ K of course). In fact, North plays ♦ 9, so the declarer plays ♦ Q from the dummy, losing to ♦ K from South. Tricks: 4–2 E/W.

Trick 7: The declarer cannot lose any other trick now as he holds the master card in spades (♠ K), the master in clubs (♣ A), the only trumps and the only diamonds. He could lay down his cards and claim the rest, as Bridge players put it. However, this is not a good idea for beginners, as discussions will ensue as to whether the claimant is certain to win all the tricks, and sometimes it will prove that he isn't. So it is as well to play the tricks out.

At trick 7, let us say South leads the ♣ K. The declarer wins with ♣ A, North plays ♣ 3 and the dummy ♣ 8. Tricks: 5–2 E/W.

From now on, with the lead shown first, the play could be:

Trick 8: W ♠ K; N ♠ 7; E ♦ 2; S ♠ 2. Tricks: 6–2 E/W

Trick 9: W ♥ J; N ♣ 6; E ♥ 8; S ♠ 3. Tricks: 7–2 E/W

Trick 10: W ♦ 7; N ♣ 7; E ♦ 6; S ♠ 6. Tricks: 8−2 E/W

Trick 11: W ♦ 5; N ♣ 9; E ♦ 8; S ♣ 5. Tricks: 9−2 E/W

Trick 12: E ♥ 10; S ♠ 9; W ♥ 5; N ♠ 8. Tricks: 10−2 E/W

Trick 13: E ♣ J; S ♠ J; W ♥ 6; N ♠ 10. Tricks: 11−2 E/W

East/West have made their contract of 4 ♥ with an overtrick. The players agree the score and enter it appropriately. As East/West made their contract, its value, 120 points, is entered below the line. The overtrick, which scores 30, is entered above the line. In fact, experienced players in this case will put the whole 150 below the line, as the score represents game. Whatever is entered below the line, another line is drawn below it to signify the end of the first game. The score sheet being kept by the East and West players will appear as in Figure 18. The score sheet kept by North and South will have the scores reversed of course, with the scores under 'They' instead of 'We'.

As this was the first game of the rubber, both sides were not vulnerable, but by winning the first game East/West are now vulnerable. This means that any penalties they incur from now on will be higher, but so will slam bonuses and overtricks made in a doubled contract.

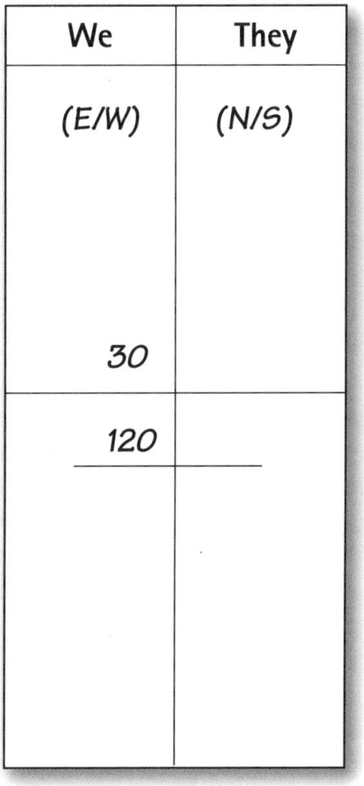

We	They
(E/W)	(N/S)
30	
120	

18
The score sheet of East after the first hand of the specimen rubber.

continued on page 40

♠
♥
♦
♣

JARGON-BUSTER

Auction After the cards are dealt and before play begins, the auction is when the players bid to establish the contract.

Bid A bid states that the player and his partner undertake to win a specified number of tricks in that hand. The last bid determines the contract.

Bidding Another term for the auction.

Call A bid or pass in the auction.

Contract An undertaking to win a specified number of tricks in a hand.

Declarer The player who first bid the suit in the contract.

Defenders The two players playing against the declarer and trying to prevent the contract being made.

Discard To lay down any card (except a trump) when the player cannot follow suit to the card led.

Double A call made during the auction whereby a player confident of beating his opponents' contract can double the penalty his opponents will concede if they fail to make their contract.

Dummy The hand of cards held by the declarer's partner, which is placed face-up on the table and played by the declarer along with his own hand.

Game A phase of Bridge to win which requires a score of 100 points, made in one or more hands.

Game contract A contract which, if won, will score enough points to win a game.

Grand slam The making of all 13 tricks in a hand, or a contract to do so.

Hand The 13 cards which are dealt to each player before play begins.

Honour cards The top five cards in each suit – the Ace, King, Queen, Jack and 10.

Lead The first card played to a trick.

Major suit The major suits are spades and hearts; the ranking is used for bidding and scoring.

Minor suit The minor suits are diamonds and clubs.

No-trumps A contract to win the majority of tricks without there being a trump suit.

Non-vulnerable A side that has not yet won a game (see 'Vulnerable').

Opening bid The first proper bid in the auction, not including passes.

Opening lead The first card to be played to the first trick, played by the person on the declarer's left.

Overtricks Any tricks won over the number specified in the contract.

Part-score Points made from a successful contract which are below the 100 necessary to constitute a game.

Pass The call a player makes when he feels his hand cannot justify a bid (also referred to as 'no bid').

Redouble A call made by a player whose side's bid has been doubled, but who is still confident of winning the contract. If successful, the side scores four times the usual points at stake for that hand.

Response A bid made in reply to a partner's opening bid.

Rubber A set of three games. To win a rubber, a team needs to win two of the three games.

Side suit A suit that is not trumps.

Small slam The making of 12 tricks in a hand, or a contract to do so.

Trick A set of four cards, one played by each player, which is won by the highest card played in the suit led, or by the highest trump. Thirteen tricks constitute a hand.

Trump A card of the suit specified as trumps during the auction, and outranks any card of the other suits.

Vulnerable A side that has won a game is said to be vulnerable, and faces higher penalties for failure to make a contact.

The second hand

When everybody is happy, the next deal can commence. West is dealer, as the deal passes clockwise. The cards just used are collected together and handed to East to shuffle while West is dealing. North now places the cards that he shuffled during the previous deal face down before South, who cuts them in two piles. West reverses the order of the piles and, taking the cards into his hand, proceeds to deal.

The hands are dealt as in Figure 19, which also includes the bidding.

We have not yet studied bidding techniques, but a rough explanation of the bidding on this hand is as follows. West, North and East do not believe their hands strong enough to open the bidding. South, who has a good hand, decides to open with 1 ♠. West doubles (see page 20), not because he has a good spade suit and expects to defeat a contract in spades, but to suggest to his partner that if his partner is strong in any of the other three suits, then he has support for him. North, with a terrible hand, passes again, and East dutifully tells his partner he has something in diamonds by bidding 2 ♦. When South and West pass again, neither unhappy with the idea of East trying to make eight tricks with diamonds as trumps, North decides that if neither East nor West is particularly strong (both passed originally) he will try a bid of 2 ♠, since he has, after all, five cards of

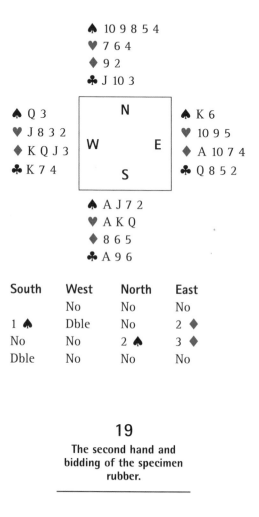

19
The second hand and bidding of the specimen rubber.

what would be his partner's trump suit if all passed. East, thinking that nearly all of North/South's strength must be in spades, ups his bid to 3 ♦, and South, who would hold five top tricks in the outside suits (if none were trumped) decides to double.

Getting to know Bridge

All pass, so East, whose side is vulnerable, has to make his contract of 3 ♦ doubled. Notice that 3 ♦, not normally enough for game, would win the second game and the rubber for East/West if he was successful.

Trick 1: South, with his strong outside hand, leads with a trump, the ♦ 5, to reduce the number of East/West's trumps. The dummy is set on the table. The declarer plays the dummy's ♦ K, with the ♦ 2 and ♦ 4 following. Tricks: 1–0 to E/W.

Trick 2: East, seeing the prospect of being able to trump only in spades, where he can lose only one trick anyway (he has the ♠ K and the dummy has the ♠ Q), decides to draw two more rounds of trumps, so leads ♦ Q from the dummy, followed by ♦ 9, ♦ 7 and ♦ 6. Tricks: 2–0 to E/W.

Trick 3: East leads ♦ 3 from the dummy, followed by ♠ 4 (a discard from North), ♦ A and ♦ 8. The defence now has no trumps, while the declarer and dummy hold one each. Tricks: 3–0 to E/W.

Trick 4: East now leads ♠ 6, which South ducks (see page 131), declining to take his ♠ A and saving it for later by playing ♠ 2. The ♠ Q and ♠ 5 follow. The dummy's Queen of course wins the trick. Tricks: 4–0 to E/W.

Trick 5: East leads ♣ K from the dummy, followed by ♣ 3, ♣ 2 and ♣ 6. Once again South ducks. The declarer has two more tricks certainly to come, and needs to make two others for his contract. Tricks: 5–0 to E/W. But...

Trick 6: East leads ♣ 7 from the dummy, covered by ♣ 10 from North. If East plays his ♣ Q, it will almost certainly lose to South's ♣ A, so East plays low with ♣ 5, hoping that South might have only ♣ A, and will have to play it on his partner's winning ♣ 10. This would make East's ♣ Q the highest left in the suit, and another winner for him. Unfortunately South plays ♣ 9. Tricks: 5–1 to E/W.

Trick 7: North now leads ♥ 4, East plays ♥ 5. South follows with ♥ A, and West with ♥ 2. Tricks: 5–2 to E/W.

Trick 8: South leads ♥ K, followed by ♥ 3, ♥ 6 and ♥ 9. Tricks: 5–3 to E/W.

Trick 9: South leads ♥ Q, followed by ♥ 8, ♥ 7 and ♥ 10. Tricks: 5–4 to E/W.

Trick 10: South leads ♠ A, followed by ♠ 3, ♠ 8 and ♠ K. This trick means the declarer's contract has failed, as he can now make no more than eight tricks. Tricks: 5–5.

Trick 11: South leads ♣ A, followed by ♣ 4, ♣ J and ♣ 8. Tricks: 6–5 to N/S.

Tricks 12, 13: As South and North have only spades left, and East and West have a trump each, East/West make the last two tricks. Tricks: 7–6 to E/W.

East/West therefore fail by two tricks to make their contract, and moreover are vulnerable and doubled. West's initial double and East's bid of 3 ♦ turned out to be very rash. They bid very badly. Had North/South been left with their bid of 2 ♠, East/West would have been successful and no doubt scored an overtrick, giving them 60 points below the line as a part-score, and 30 above.

As it happens, East/West's decision to bid higher and their failure to land the contract left North/South with a score of 500 points above the line. The new East/West score sheet is shown in Figure 20.

The third hand
When the four score sheets are completed (one by each of the players), North deals the next hand, taking the cards which East has shuffled and West has cut, as described before. Figure 21 shows the deal.

Nobody has much more than an average hand here. North passes, as does East. South has a poor hand and passes, and West, without a strong suit, has to do the same. All of the players throw in their hands, and West begins to shuffle this pack for the next hand.

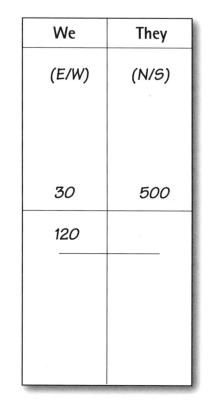

We	They
(E/W)	(N/S)
30	500
120	

20
The score sheet of East
after the second hand of
the specimen rubber.

The fourth hand
East takes the cards which North cuts after South has finished shuffling. East deals the next hand, resulting in the hands as shown in Figure 22.

East has an above-average hand and opens with a bid of 1 ♦. South passes,

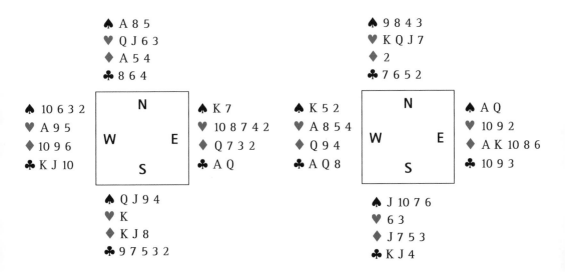

	♠ A 8 5		♠ 9 8 4 3
	♥ Q J 6 3		♥ K Q J 7
	♦ A 5 4		♦ 2
	♣ 8 6 4		♣ 7 6 5 2

♠ 10 6 3 2   N   ♠ K 7   ♠ K 5 2   N   ♠ A Q
♥ A 9 5   W   E   ♥ 10 8 7 4 2   ♥ A 8 5 4   W   E   ♥ 10 9 2
♦ 10 9 6   S   ♦ Q 7 3 2   ♦ Q 9 4   S   ♦ A K 10 8 6
♣ K J 10   ♣ A Q   ♣ A Q 8   ♣ 10 9 3

	♠ Q J 9 4		♠ J 10 7 6
	♥ K		♥ 6 3
	♦ K J 8		♦ J 7 5 3
	♣ 9 7 5 3 2		♣ K J 4

21
The third hand of the specimen rubber, in which all passed.

South	West	North	East
			1 ♦
No	1 ♥	No	2 ♦
No	3 NT		

and West, who has a good hand himself, bids 1 ♥, telling his partner of his four-card major suit (how this tells his partner is explained later). North passes, and East, with moderate support for hearts, repeats his diamond bid, his 2 ♦ telling his partner that diamonds is his only suit longer than four cards.

South passes, and West, realizing his side has much of the balance of power, and with his all-round balanced hand, decides to bid game at 3NT, despite the previous overbidding. All pass, and 3NT, played by West, is the contract.

22
The fourth hand and bidding of the specimen rubber.

Trick 1: North leads the ♥ K, and dummy is set on the table. Declarer chooses the ♥ 2 to follow, and when South plays ♥ 3, ducks by playing ♥ 4 from his hand. He does not want to play ♥ A, because it would weaken his position in hearts and it is just possible that North could have ♥ Q, ♥ J and another heart.

West can see he is now certain of eight tricks (♠ A, K, Q, ♥ A, ♦ A, K, Q and ♣ A) and sure of making a ninth, and possibly tenth, in diamonds with the ♣ Q a possibility for another. Tricks: 1–0 to N/S.

Trick 2: North follows with ♥ Q, on which are played ♥ 9, 6 and 5. The declarer has ducked again, as he can see that North can hold no better than ♥ J and 7 now, and that he cannot lead them again without presenting two heart tricks to declarer with ♥ A and 8. Tricks: 2–0 to N/S.

Trick 3: North decides to switch, and chooses ♠ 3, hoping that his partner might hold ♠ K and force the declarer into an early choice whether to play ♠ A or ♠ Q. The declarer plays ♠ A from the dummy, on which the ♠ 6 and ♠ 2 follow. Tricks: 2–1 to N/S.

Trick 4: The declarer now tests the diamonds. He plays ♦ A from the dummy, which is followed by ♦ 3, ♦ 4 and ♦ 2. Tricks: 2–2.

Trick 5: The declarer leads ♦ 6 from the dummy, followed by ♦ 5 and ♦ Q, with North discarding ♣ 2. The declarer now realizes that ♦ J is in South's hand and is a winner for South. Tricks: 3–2 to E/W.

Trick 6: Because the declarer needs a fourth diamond to make the contract, he leads ♦ 9 from his hand, followed by ♣ 5, ♦ K and ♦ 7. Tricks: 4–2 to E/W.

Trick 7: The declarer leads ♦ 10 from the dummy, followed by South's ♦ J, the declarer's discard of ♥ 8 and North's ♣ 6. Tricks: 4–3 to E/W.

Trick 8: South leads ♠ 7, which is followed by ♠ 5, ♠ 4 and ♠ Q. Tricks: 5–3 to E/W.

Trick 9: The declarer now leads and makes the last diamond, ♦ 8, followed by three discards, ♣ 4, ♣ 8 and ♣ 7. Tricks: 6–3 to E/W.

Trick 10: The declarer leads ♣ 3 from dummy, upon which South plays ♣ J. The declarer plays ♣ Q here, in the hope of making an extra trick. Even if North held the ♣ K, declarer would make the last three tricks for his contract because he holds the master cards in all three suits still in play. As it happens ♣ Q wins, as North discards ♠ 8. Tricks: 7–3 to E/W.

Tricks 11, 12, 13: The declarer plays ♣ A, ♥ A and ♠ K to win the last three tricks, making ten tricks in all and his contract. Tricks: 10–3 to E/W.

So East/West score 100 for game below the line and 30 for the extra trick above the line. This is usually written as 130 below the line, as the game, and indeed the rubber, is now complete. For winning the rubber by two games to nil, East/West score a bonus of 700 above the line. The final score sheet is shown in Figure 23, with East/West winners by 980–500, or 480, points.

Summing up

You have now learned the basic principles of Bridge. You know about the pack, the suits and how they rank, how to decide on partners and where to sit, how shuffling and dealing are arranged, how to sort out your hand, what is meant by tricks and what trumps are.

You have been given an outline of how the bidding works and how the cards are played. You have also been shown how hands and the bidding in Bridge are generally set out in newspapers, magazines and books.

This chapter contained a long section on the scoring in Bridge. At first glance, this would have seemed complex and off-putting but, as explained, it is not necessary to memorize all this before starting to play. Think of all the millions of people who play cricket and football without being completely au fait with all of the rules. You will soon pick up the essential elements of scoring at Bridge, and the rest can always be looked up as the need arises. Some packs of playing cards even include a spare card on which is set out the basic scoring, and you can always refer to

We	They
(E/W)	*(N/S)*
700	
30	*500*
120	
130	
980	*500*

23
The score sheet of East after the final hand of the specimen rubber.

pages 152–153 for a quick answer to any scoring queries.

With all this new information at your command, we have run through a typical specimen rubber to give you the feel of how the game is played. No doubt you will still have questions, such as, 'But I don't quite see how during the auction players arrive at the best contract to play in.' Well, players do not always arrive at the best contract, and even experts get into a mix-up at times. But that is part of the game, and the next parts of this book will look at how the bidding is conducted and how to make the best of your chances in the play itself.

Summing up

♠
♥
♦
♣

QUICK REFERENCE GUIDE

STARTING OUT

Bridge is based on playing **tricks** and **bidding** on the likely outcome of **tricks**. The highest card in the suit of the **lead** card wins, except where a **trump** is played.

Key points
- Four people play with one pack of shuffled cards, no jokers.
- Two teams of two are known as North/South and East/West.
- Partners sit opposite each other, matching the compass co-ordinates.

DRAW AND DEAL

Each player picks a card. The two with the highest cards become partners and the one with the highest card deals. Dealer gives each player 13 cards, dealt one at a time in clockwise direction.

Key points
- One **hand** (deal) is 13 cards for each player.
- Cards in descending order are: A, K, Q, J, 10, 9, 8, 7, 6, 5, 4, 3, 2.
- Suits in descending order are: Spades, Hearts, Diamonds, Clubs.

SORT

The aim is to see at a glance what cards of each suit have been dealt. Make a fan, alternating black and red suits, and placing cards in descending order with highest on left, lowest on right.

Key points
- Cards are never picked up until all the cards are dealt.
- Suggested sort order, left to right: Spades, Hearts, Clubs, Diamonds.
- With experience, vary this to prevent opponents making deductions about your hand.

AUCTION OR BIDDING

After the deal, before play starts, players bid to establish a **contract:** an undertaking to win a specified number of **tricks** in that **hand**. The aim is to reach a **contract** that suits the combined **hands** of the team.

Key points
- Each player **calls** in turn, starting with the dealer and proceeding clockwise.

- Partners cannot see each other's hands, but make inferences from the bids.
- **Trump** suit: chosen in the auction, and outranks other suits.
- Lowest possible bid is 'one club', the highest bid is 'seven no-trumps **redoubled**'.

CALLING THE BID

The first player making a bid states which suit will be **trumps** or that **hand** will be played with no trumps and states the number of **tricks** above six their side proposes to make. Other players in turn **call** in response.

Key points
- Each bid must overbid the previous bid. For example, 1 ♣ can be overbid by 1 ♦, 1 ♦ by 1 ♥ and so on.
- If player has a poor hand, he can '**pass**' or '**no bid**'.
- **Bidding** ends when three players have passed consecutively.
- Team that made the last bid has 'bought the **contract**'.

THE PLAY

The player on the contracting side who first bid the suit of the contract is called the **declarer**. The player to the left of the **declarer** lays the **lead** card in the first **trick**. The **dummy** is laid and the **trick** is completed in a clockwise direction.

Key points
- 13 tricks are played until the **hand** is finished.
- Winner of a trick leads to the next **trick**.
- Points are allocated at the end of the **hand**.

SCORING

To win overall, a team must win a **rubber**: (three **games**, unless the first two are won by same team). A **game** is a **hand** or hands where 100 points are scored. See quick reference scoring guide on pages 152–153

Key points
- Points for winning a **contract** are scored **below the line** and count towards winning **games** and **rubbers**.
- Any extra or other points count towards settlement at the end and are scored **above the line**.
- Penalties are points awarded to the opponents. See page 32.
- Bonuses are extra points awarded to teams. See page 35.

THE
BIDDING

2

THE BIDDING

You now know the mechanics of how to play Bridge. But knowing how it all works is a long way from actually sitting down and playing it. You know what is meant by the auction, or the bidding, but once you are seated at the table, the cards are dealt, you have picked up and sorted your hand, what do you do next? The first thing is to decide whether or not you have a good hand. This is really where the game starts.

Evaluating the hand

There is more than one way of valuing your hand, but almost everybody uses a point count. This is a method whereby Aces and picture cards are allocated points. It was publicized by an American Bridge-player, writer and lawmaker very influential in the 1920s, named Milton Work. If you hear Bridge players describe a hand as having so many points or read about a point count, a high-card point count or a Work point count, it is this system that is being referred to.

It is very simple. It values high cards as follows:

Ace = 4 points
King = 3 points
Queen = 2 points
Jack = 1 point

Some hand valuations are given in Figures 24 to 27 (see pages 53 and 54).

MILTON WORK

Milton Work (1864–1943) was a remarkable man. Born in Philadelphia, he was a talented athlete, reaching high standards in baseball, golf, tennis and cricket. A lawyer, he devoted his life to Bridge from 1917, and had a hand in developing the laws. He did not actually invent the Work count, but his name became associated with it after he advocated it in his writings. In 1928 he was paid $7,000 per week, a huge sum then, to lecture on Bridge on the Vaudeville circuit (the US equivalent of the British music halls). In 1897 he toured England as manager of the Philadelphians cricket team, who played 15 first-class matches and actually beat Warwickshire and Sussex, who had the great Ranji in their team.

Since there are four Aces, four Kings, four Queens and four Jacks in a pack of cards, the total number of points in a pack is 40. Therefore, if your hand contains ten points it is an average hand. If it contains more, you have a better than average hand; if fewer, a worse than average hand.

This might seem to you surprisingly rough-and-ready for what you've probably regarded as a very skilful game. It is, but in practice is extremely useful, and even world champions use it. You cannot really play Bridge, or understand Bridge columns in newspapers, without knowing about the point count.

Of course, it does not tell you everything about the value of your hand. Some experts have refined it to take account of the shape of the hand, adding points for length or shortage in a suit (see panel). We will keep things simpler here. However, you do need to appreciate and to estimate the value of the shape of a hand, or, as it is also called, its *distribution*.

Distribution

Bridge players describe the distribution of the hand by stating the number of cards in each suit, starting with the longest suit and ending with the shortest. For example, a 6–4–2–1 hand has six cards of one suit, four of another, two of another and one of the other; a 4–4–3–2 means two suits of

four cards, one of three and one of two. Note that the 4–4–3–2 is not in the order of spades, hearts, diamonds, clubs (the order of precedence of the suits). The longest suit comes first, so the 4–4–3–2 might be clubs, hearts, diamonds, spades.

There are three basic descriptions of the shape of a hand. A *balanced* hand is one with a shape of 4–3–3–3 (the most balanced you can get) or 4–4–3–2 or 5–3–3–2. An *unbalanced* hand is one that contains a *void* (not having any cards in a particular suit) or a *singleton* (one card only in a suit). Examples of unbalanced hands are 4–4–4–1,

♠
♥
♦
♣

7–3–2–1, 6–4–3–0. Hands that fall between these extremes might be called *semi-balanced*. These are hands that do not contain a void or singleton, but have two or more *doubletons* (suits of two cards only). For example, hand shapes of 7–2–2–2, 6–3–2–2 and 5–4–2–2 could be called semi-balanced.

One, two or three-suited

Another way of describing shape refers to the number of good or, more precisely, *biddable* suits. A biddable suit is one that contains four cards. If you hold Ace, King, Queen only in a suit,

clearly that is a good suit, but you would not open the bidding with it. At least one of your other suits must contain four cards or more, and that suit would be regarded as the more biddable. As we shall see, to open the bidding in a suit promises your partner at least four cards in that suit.

A hand, therefore, that contains only one suit of four cards or more, say 5–3–2–2, would be called a one-suiter. A hand with two suits of four or more, say 6–4–2–1, would be a two-suiter, and a hand with three suits of at least four cards would be a three-suiter. This could only be 4–4–4–1 or 5–4–4–0.

These descriptions of shape are to help you learn when and how to bid – they are not part of the rules of Bridge.

Distribution and bidding

The distribution of your hand will affect your bidding. A balanced hand is best for no-trump contracts, since you do not have a short suit in which you are likely to be able to trump. You will be following suit to most leads. An unbalanced hand suggests a trump contract would be better. A void or a singleton gives you the opportunity to use a trump on the first or second round of that suit. And, of course, if you have a five or six-card suit which you can nominate as trumps you are in a powerful position. A semi-balanced hand might be suitable for a trump or a no-trump contract.

DISTRIBUTION PROBABILITIES

• • • • • • • • • • • • • • • • • • •

There are 39 possible hand patterns in Bridge, the most frequent being a 4–4–3–2 distribution, the most rare the freak 13–0–0–0. On average, the 4–4–3–2 pattern will occur in 21.6 per cent of hands – more than one in five. The next four most frequent distributions are: 5–3–3–2, 5–4–3–1, 5–4–2–2 and 4–3–3–3. Between them these five patterns will occur in over 70 per cent of hands.

Points and distribution combined

The instant way to evaluate your hand is to look at it in terms of both high-card points and distribution. Four examples of hands are shown in Figures 24 to 27 (see below and page 54), and you might regard them as follows.

Look at the hand shown in Figure 24. If you have a long suit, headed by high cards, it is a very powerful weapon. This unbalanced hand contains above-average points with its feature the strong spade suit. You have six spades, the other three hands together have only seven. If spades were trumps, and neither opponent held four of the seven missing spades, you could lead the Ace, King, Queen in turn to remove

your opponent's spades and are certain to make six tricks from the suit. The singleton heart is also valuable, as it means you can trump a second round of hearts, and the clubs should provide a couple of tricks if your partner holds Ace or King, so you evaluate this hand as '12 points, a strong major suit and good distribution' – that is, it is better than many other 12-point hands.

The hand in Figure 25 also has a good distribution. Unless clubs are trumps your void in that suit means that you can trump a club lead the first time round. So although your hand has only an average ten points, it is an interesting hand, and if the auction suggests your partner has strength in any of the other three suits, you might

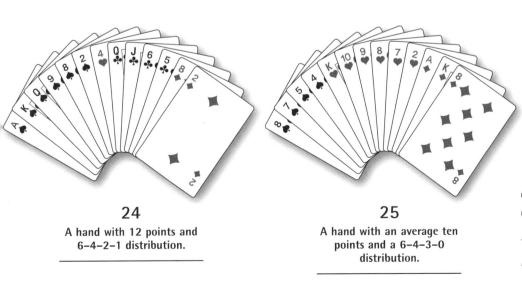

24
A hand with 12 points and 6–4–2–1 distribution.

25
A hand with an average ten points and a 6–4–3–0 distribution.

between you have hands sufficient to score a game. It is not a hand you would usually open the bidding with, as we shall see later.

Similarly, Figure 26 has a strong distribution, making it worth more than its 14 points. Bridge players would call it a good two-suiter, as all its strength lies in two suits, the spades and diamonds. If your partner has support for you in either of these suits (say three or four cards) and in addition has the Ace of hearts or clubs you could have the makings of a small slam. However, hands like this do depend on a *fit* with your partner, who, of course, is more likely to hold a collection of mostly hearts and clubs, in which case you will have to take care not to bid too highly.

The opposite type of hand is shown in Figure 27, which has a balanced distribution – players also call it a *flat* distribution. The suits could not be more evenly distributed than 4-3-3-3. It is an uninteresting hand, and if you picked it up you would only be bidding in response to your partner – you wouldn't dream of opening the bidding yourself with a hand like this.

Values for game

Now that you have an idea of how to rate your hand, we should consider what sort of values are required to make a game, which you will remember requires your side to make a score of 100 points. This score can be reached by making a contract of 3NT (exactly 100

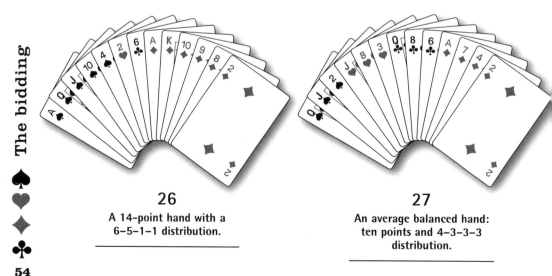

26
A 14-point hand with a
6–5–1–1 distribution.

27
An average balanced hand:
ten points and 4-3-3-3
distribution.

points), 4 ♠ or 4 ♥ (120 points), or 5 ♦ or 5 ♣ (again exactly 100 points). It follows that to make a game in no-trumps you need 9 of the 13 tricks; you need 10 in a major suit and 11 in a minor suit. It is clearly difficult to make a game in clubs or diamonds as you can afford to lose only two tricks.

Game in no-trumps As a guide, it is estimated that a combined high-card point count of 25 points or more is required to make a game in no-trumps. This does not mean, of course, that if you have, say, 28 points you are more or less guaranteed to make 3NT. You need to have, between you, high cards in all four suits. If between you you have a weak suit, for example neither of you has more than three cards and the highest is the Jack, your opponents could make three or four tricks in it before you even get started.

Game in a major suit Generally a combined count of 26 points and eight or more trumps is required to give you a good chance of success.

Game in a minor suit You will need about 29 points plus eight or more trumps to have a chance of making game. Sometimes a solid minor suit in one hand (say seven or eight cards headed by Ace, King, Queen) plays better as a no-trump contract, if all of the other three suits are *guarded* (that is,

they contain *stopper* high cards which prevent the opposition winning several tricks in the suit before you can obtain the lead yourself).

Values for slams
To make a grand slam (all 13 tricks) you require as a partnership around 37 points and 8 trumps. This is a tall order, as it means that your opponents cannot hold more than a King, or otherwise a Queen plus Jack, between them. Of course, if your opponents hold an Ace (and neither you nor your partner is void in the suit) they can destroy your hopes with the opening lead.

To make a small slam (12 tricks), you will need about 33 points and 8 trumps for success.

Bidding as a partnership
You have evaluated your hand, and you are going to bid. You will recall that earlier in this book it was stated that bidding is like conducting a conversation with your partner while listening to the conversation between your opponents. Therefore each bid you make should convey something to your partner, and his bids should convey something to you.

The problem is that there are is a certain number of words you are allowed to say. You can say the seven numbers from one to seven. Whichever number you choose will be coupled either with one of the four suits or with

♠
♥
♦
♣

the words 'no-trumps'. That makes 13 words. You can also say 'double', 'redouble' and whatever phrase you use to indicate you do not wish to make a bid: 'pass', 'no' or 'no bid'. That makes a grand total of 16 or 17 words that you are allowed to say. You are not allowed to make any gestures or put any inflection in your voice that might convey information. This would be cheating. 'I'll try a dodgy two spades,' is not the language of Bridge.

So how do you describe coherently to your partner which one of the approximately 635 billion possible Bridge hands you hold?

Bidding systems

The answer to the question of how to convey information in the auction is bidding systems. There have been any number of systems invented of which probably the best known and most widely used is the Acol system. There have been many variations made by players to the basic Acol system (not surprisingly, as it was invented about 70 years ago) but its ideas have stood the test of time and are used and understood by most players. Bidding advice in this book is based upon it.

You must remember that what you bid is entirely up to you. Sometimes beginners make the mistake of thinking that because they have a hand of a certain type, they *have* to make a

certain bid. You will hear remarks like, 'I had 13 points in my hand, so I had to open the bidding.' There is no compulsion. The bidding system is to help you convey information to your partner. You need not be a slave to it, but remember that if you deviate from it recklessly you could be confusing your partner, which is not a good idea. Needless to say, you and your partner must agree on the system you are going to use and what is meant by the bids each of you makes.

ACOL SYSTEM

The Acol system, the standard system of bidding in Britain and widely used elsewhere, is named after a road in Hampstead, North London in which stood a small Bridge-club where the system was developed in 1934. Its originators were a group of famous players and writers who included Maurice Harrison-Gray, Terence Reese, J.C.H. Marx, S.J. Simon and one-time Chancellor of the Exchequer Iain MacLeod.

Your opponents, too, are entitled to know what system you are using. This will not be a problem at the learning stages but, at the highest levels of competitive Bridge, players must state their systems, and if a player is puzzled by a bid by an opponent at any time in the bidding, he is entitled to ask the bidder's partner what he understood by the bid. Of course, the opponent might be as puzzled as the player who asked the question, but he must answer!

Types of bid

Bids can be divided into two types. *Natural bids* are those in which the bidder names the suit or suits where his strength lies, with a view to playing the contract in such a suit. The majority of bids are of this type. There is another type, however, called a *conventional bid* or an *artificial bid*. These bids mean something quite unrelated to the suit being bid. The best known is probably the opening bid of 2 ♣, which merely tells partner that you have a very powerful hand of 23 points or more. Clubs need not have anything to do with it. These bids will be discussed later. Do not worry – there are not many of them, and they are very easy to learn.

When to open the bidding

You should remember that when you bid you are conveying a message to your partner about your hand. What you can convey is limited because, as mentioned earlier, you have only 16 or 17 words at your disposal, but if you and your partner understand each other it is surprising how much you can manage. Perhaps the most important thing is not to mislead your partner. Suppose you are thinking of bidding 1 ♥. You should have in the back of your mind the thought, 'What sort of hand will my partner think I hold if I bid 1 ♥?' If your partner couldn't possible equate the bid with your hand, then you should be bidding something else, or not bidding at all.

You should consider opening the bidding if you have 12 or more high-card points. With good distribution you could open the bidding with 11 points. You should almost certainly open the bidding if you have 13 points or more. With 12 points, the pattern of the hand might be the deciding factor.

The reasoning behind this is as follows. If you hold 13 points, your partner needs to hold only 8 points for your side to hold the balance of power, there being 40 points in the pack. Should your partner hold 12 points or more, there is a prospect that you can make game. So it is worth making an opening bid, and beginning the dialogue with your partner.

♠
♥
♦
♣

Opening bids of one in a suit

At least three-quarters of opening bids in Bridge are of One in a suit. The range of points for which this is an apt opening is wide, from 11 to 19.

You might open with only 11 points if you held a strong six-card suit, or with two five-card suits. Figures 28 and 29 are examples of these. Without these strong distributions, it is unwise to open with 11 points, bearing in mind your partner will be expecting 13 or more.

To open with 12 points, you need a good five or six-card suit, preferably a major. Figures 30 and 31 are hands of 12 points on which you could open. With 13 points or more, you should open with your longest suit. Figures 32 and 33 are such hands.

Not opening with 13 points

Occasionally you might hold a hand with 13 points, three above average, where it is advisable to pass. Such hands might hold the high cards in short suits, leading to no suit being very strong in itself. If in addition the best is a minor suit, restraint could be the best policy. If your partner has the strength to open the bidding then you can respond by showing your strength. If, on the other hand, your opponents win the contract, then you have strength that might defeat them. Figure 34 (see page 60) is a hand where discretion might pay off.

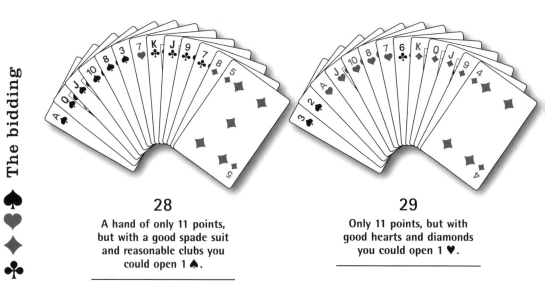

28
A hand of only 11 points, but with a good spade suit and reasonable clubs you could open 1 ♠.

29
Only 11 points, but with good hearts and diamonds you could open 1 ♥.

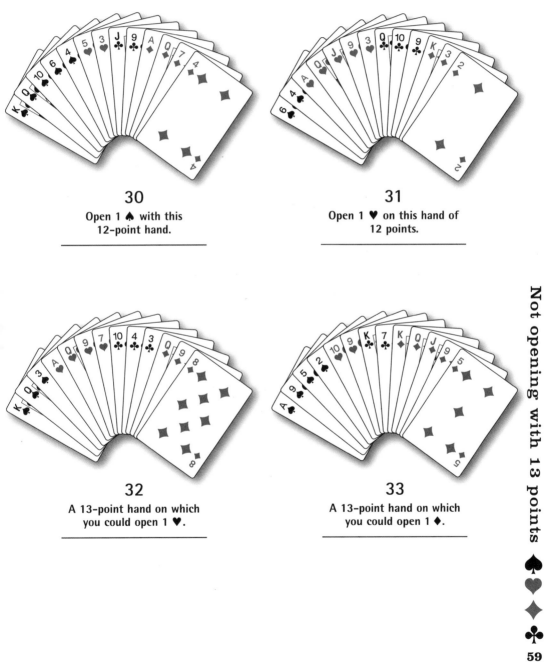

30

Open 1 ♠ with this
12-point hand.

31

Open 1 ♥ on this hand of
12 points.

32

A 13-point hand on which
you could open 1 ♥.

33

A 13-point hand on which
you could open 1 ♦.

Not opening with 13 points ♠ ♥ ♦ ♣

Opening with a choice of suits

Always open with your longest suit, but if you hold two five-card suits or two or more four-card suits, of similar strength to each other, bid the suit that gives you and your partner the most bidding room. For example, if you hold long suits in hearts and diamonds, it is usually better to bid the hearts first. This is because if your partner responds with 1 ♠ or 2 ♣, you can then bid 2 ♦, thus giving your partner all the information you can while still at the Two level. If his strongest suits are spades and clubs, it is clear to him that your hands do not fit very well together and you can sign off before getting into too high a contract.

If on the other hand you decide to open the bidding with equal length in, say, spades and clubs, it is wiser to open with 1 ♣, allowing your partner to respond in diamonds or hearts while still giving you the opportunity to mention your spades at the One level.

Figures 35 to 37 show hands of two or more four or five-card suits, and the recommended opening bid.

With two five-card suits it is better to bid the higher-ranking first, irrespective of their relative strengths, as in Figure 38.

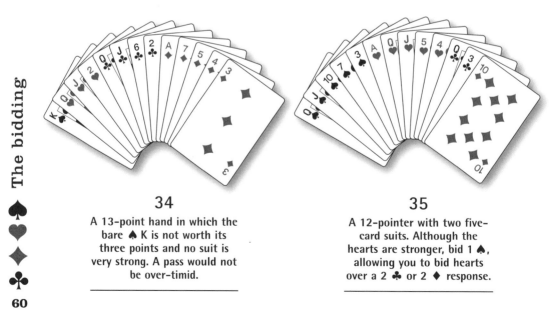

34

A 13-point hand in which the bare ♠ K is not worth its three points and no suit is very strong. A pass would not be over-timid.

35

A 12-pointer with two five-card suits. Although the hearts are stronger, bid 1 ♠, allowing you to bid hearts over a 2 ♣ or 2 ♦ response.

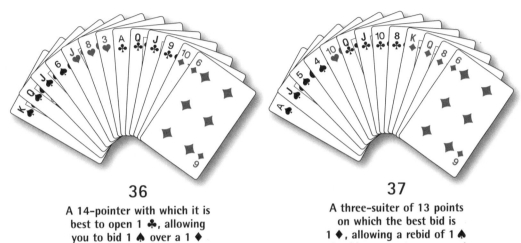

36

A 14-pointer with which it is best to open 1 ♣, allowing you to bid 1 ♠ over a 1 ♦ or 1 ♥ response.

37

A three-suiter of 13 points on which the best bid is 1 ♦, allowing a rebid of 1 ♠ should your partner respond with 1 ♥.

38

A 14-point hand with two five-card suits. Here it is better to bid the spades first with 1 ♠.

It is necessary to use discretion over following the above principles too slavishly, however. Figure 39 (see page 62) shows a case in point. With three four-card suits, the usual practice here would be to bid 1 ♠, but the spade suit is lacking in high-card point values. The diamond suit is the strongest but in this case it would be better to bid the hearts, as the higher ranking of the two best suits. You are well placed to deal with any response your partner makes: you have support if he bids spades or diamonds and a response of 2 ♣ from him would give you plenty of bidding space to find the right contract.

♠
♥
♦
♣

Another case for overlooking these concepts is where your hand is particularly strong. Figure 40 shows a 16-point hand. It is probably best here to advise your partner of your good spades. If he should bid 2 ♥ (which is likely), you have used up a lot of bidding space and bypassed your chance of bidding clubs or diamonds at the Two level, but in this case you bid 2NT, telling partner you have values in the other suits. You still have time to find the best suit for game, if game is on, with 3NT or 4 ♠.

We will discuss opening bids of more than One in a suit, and opening bids in no-trumps, a little later.

Opening bids of one in a suit: summary

Opening bids of One in a suit can be made with hands of a point count of 11 points to about 19. Usually, to open the bidding, you will have at least 13 points. The suit you will name will be your longest suit, irrespective of whether or not it is the richest in high cards. If there are two or more suits of identical length, you will name the suit that allows most space for bidding, as outlined above, but there can be exceptions to this, depending on the strengths of the suit.

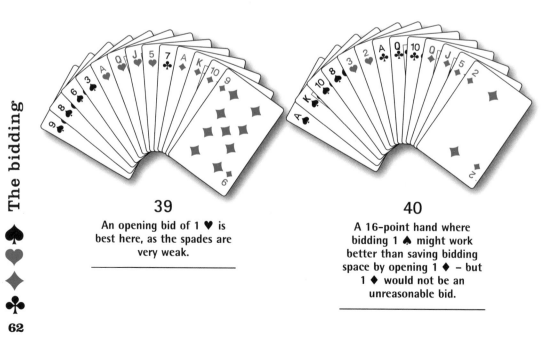

39

An opening bid of 1 ♥ is best here, as the spades are very weak.

40

A 16-point hand where bidding 1 ♠ might work better than saving bidding space by opening 1 ♦ – but 1 ♦ would not be an unreasonable bid.

Responses to opening bids of one in a suit

Your partner has bid – either 1 ♠, 1 ♥, 1 ♦ or 1 ♣. You can deduce from this that he is likely to have 13 or more high-card points, but could, with a good distribution, have as few as 11. The suit he named will be his longest suit, and therefore will include at least four cards, quite likely five. The opponent to your right has passed. You must now consider your response. We will consider this under six possibilities, which depend on the strength and type of your hand.

Denial pass

It is quite possible that your hand will be so poor that you can offer your partner very little hope of significant assistance from your hand. As a general rule, it is advisable to pass if you hold five points or fewer, unless there are distributive reasons for thinking your hand will help your partner – for instance, if you have five or six cards in his strongest suit. Bear in mind that even if your partner has 17 or 18 high-card points, a contribution of fewer than six points from your hand will not raise the combined total to the 26 points that is regarded as giving you a good chance of making game. Suppose your partner has opened the bidding with 1 ♠. Figures 41 and 42 show hands on which it would be best to pass. Even if you

41
Your partner has opened 1 ♠. With five points, you can offer no encouragement and should pass.

42
Your partner has opened 1 ♠. You hold four spades but with a mere two points should pass.

♠
♥
♦
♣

have a strongish suit of your own, which might offer you and your partner a chance of game in your best suit rather than his, it is best to pass with five points or fewer. Figure 43 shows such a situation. If your partner, who opens 1 ♥, is very strong there could even be a game for you in spades. But it would be risky to bid 1 ♠ or 1NT (a *limit* bid, see below) in this situation. It would be best to pass. There is always the possibility that the opponent on your left will *reopen the bidding* and give you the chance to mention your spades. In the meantime, a pass tells your partner not to expect more than five points from your hand.

A pass in response to an opening bid by your partner is called a *denial* bid. It denies the possibility that you hold a hand that is likely to be of any help to him in his play.

Limit bids

There are two forms of *limit* bid, which is a type of bid that gives your partner some encouragement, but tells him not to get too excited, as the support you can offer is limited. The typical high-card point count for a limited bid is 6–9 points.

Single raise   If your hand includes support for your partner's suit, you can make a single raise of his suit. For example, if your partner has opened 1 ♥, and you hold 6–9 points with four

43
Your partner has opened 1 ♥. Despite your spade suit, it is best to pass with only four points.

hearts, you bid 2 ♥. This tells your partner that you have support for his hearts and probably hold 6–9 points.

Alternatively, you might hold 6–9 points but without strong support for partner's suit. In this case bid 1NT. This tells your partner your exact situation. Examples of a single raise in partner's suit are shown in Figures 44 to 46 (see opposite and page 66).

In Figure 44 you hold four cards of your partner's suit – hearts. This means that between you you must hold at least eight trumps, if you win the contract in hearts. Your doubleton in spades suggests that you may be able to trump spades with your supporting trumps.

The hand in Figure 45 shows only three cards in the proposed trump suit of hearts, but as they include the King, the raise to 2 ♥ is justified. The hand contains nine points, and a doubleton in diamonds. It is in order to raise in your partner's suit with only three of the proposed trumps, provided one is the Queen or above. There is a risk, however, that should your partner play the contract in hearts, he might have only seven trumps at his disposal to the opponents' six.

Although the range for this bid is typically 6–9 points, you could make it with a lower point-count if your support for the trump suit is particularly good, say five cards or four headed by a King.

Figure 46 (see page 66) shows a hand of only five points, but its five cards in the potential trump suit, guaranteeing at least nine trumps in the partnership, plus its useful distribution, makes a raise justifiable.

Figure 47 shows a hand of only four points, but the strong support for hearts as trumps, and the void in spades, is enough to encourage partner with a single raise. Remember the single raise is a limited bid. Your partner will not be expecting a very strong hand, but knows that some help will be derived from the cards you hold in your hand.

44

After your partner opens
1 ♥, with seven points
and four hearts bid 2 ♥,
a single raise.

45

Respond 2 ♥ to partner's
opening 1 ♥. Although you
hold only three hearts, one is
the King and you have nine
points.

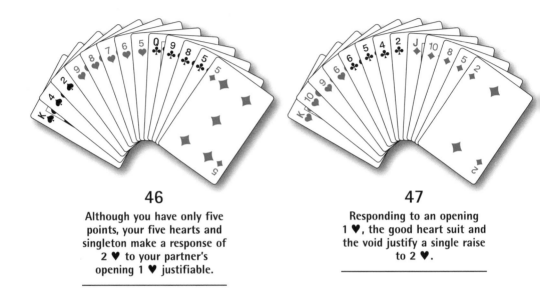

46

Although you have only five
points, your five hearts and
singleton make a response of
2 ♥ to your partner's
opening 1 ♥ justifiable.

47

Responding to an opening
1 ♥, the good heart suit and
the void justify a single raise
to 2 ♥.

Raise to 1NT The second form of
limited bid is to raise to 1NT. Like the
single raise, this also promises 6–9
high-card points. The difference is that
the raise to 1NT does not promise trump
support, but rather a balanced hand. For
this reason, one should not take liberties
with the point count. If you respond
1NT to your partner's opening bid, he
will expect 6–9 high-card points, and
will complain if he finds your hand has
only 5. He is not expecting much in
trumps. Figure 48 shows the minimum
required for a raise of 1NT over an
opening bid of 1 ♠. The maximum
hand for a bid of 1NT is shown in
Figure 49.

48

A minimum hand (six points)
for a response of 1NT to
your partner's opening 1 ♠.

49
Opposite an opening bid of 1 ♠, respond 1NT. The nine points held is the top end of the range for this bid.

50
Your partner has opened 1 ♠. To mention your good hearts, requiring a bid at the Two level, is not justified with only seven points. 1NT is the best response.

In Figure 50, you hold a balanced hand of seven points, but with a five-card heart suit headed by King and Jack, which would be worth mentioning, and should be if it were possible to do so at the level of One (that is, if the opening bid had been in diamonds or clubs). But to change the suit at the Two level requires a little more than seven points, as we shall see, so 1NT is the best response.

Because the requirement for a limited bid response to One in a suit is roughly the same 6–9 points for a single raise in the suit or for a raise to 1NT, there will be a number of hands – balanced hands with good trumps – where a fine choice

has to be made between them. The deciding factor in the choice is the strength of the trumps. Figures 51 and 52 (see page 68) both show hands of 4-3-3-3 distribution and eight points. The opening bid in each case is 1 ♠. The suits of two cards have been altered so that the spades are stronger in Figure 52 than in Figure 51. This justifies a single raise to 2 ♠ in preference to the response of 1NT.

Change of suit response
The third possibility as a response to an opening bid at the One level is a change of suit. This doesn't require a range of high-card points because a lot

♠
♥
♦
♣

51

With a balanced eight points
over your partner's opening
1 ♠, the best response is 1NT,
as spades is the weakest suit.

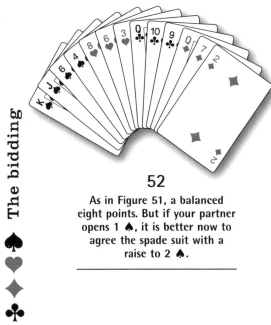

52

As in Figure 51, a balanced
eight points. But if your partner
opens 1 ♠, it is better now to
agree the spade suit with a
raise to 2 ♠.

depends on the suit and the level of the
bid needed, so it could be made from a
hand with as few as 5 points or as
many as 18.

If your partner opens the bidding
with One in a suit and you cannot
support that suit but have a good suit of
your own, you can name your suit. If it
is of four good cards (including Ace,
Jack or King, Queen), or of five or six
cards, you can respond with as few as
five high-card points. Figures 53 to 55
show some examples.

In Figures 53 and 54 you have a
good heart suit and a good spade suit
respectively, facing an opening bid of
1 ♦. In neither case is diamonds an
attractive trump suit for you. The five-
card heart suit in Figure 53, headed by
the King and with good *intermediate*
values in 10, 9, 8, is strong enough for
you to bid hearts despite the miserable
five points. In Figure 54 again you have
only five high-card points. But the
spade suit is so good, with six spades
headed by King, Jack, 10, that nobody
would blame you for bidding 1 ♠.
If your partner happens to have four
spades to the Ace you could well have
values for game.

Figure 55 shows a balanced hand
with the best suit, hearts, having only
four cards. Again you must respond to
1 ♦. Here you have some support for
diamonds: the King, 10 and 9 should be
valuable to your partner in a diamond
contract. You have nine points, the

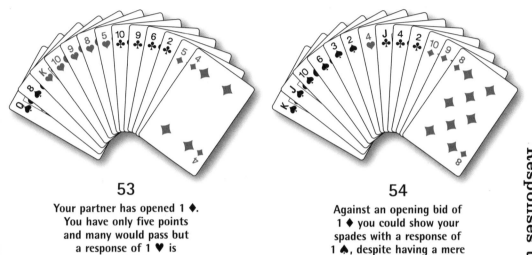

53
Your partner has opened 1 ♦.
You have only five points
and many would pass but
a response of 1 ♥ is
permissible.

54
Against an opening bid of
1 ♦ you could show your
spades with a response of
1 ♠, despite having a mere
five points.

55
Your partner has opened
1 ♦. Your heart suit is
strong enough for a
response of 1 ♥.

maximum for a raise to 2 ♦. However,
it does not take up much bidding space
to bid 1 ♥ instead and let your partner
know that you have a good heart suit.
This is the better bid.

You might well be wondering here
how it can happen that, in the
examples in Figures 53 to 55, both you
and your partner have bid, and have
bid different suits, so that you do not
know yet which will be the trump suit,
especially as in two of the examples
you have no more than five points.

There is no need for alarm, for two
reasons. The first is that neither of you
have bid above the level of One, so
there is still opportunity to find the best

♠
♥
♦
♣

suit without needing to bid so high that you are out of your depth. The second reason is that by changing the suit you have introduced a new principle to the science of good partnership bidding: the *forcing bid*.

This principle states that the opener whose partner responds by changing the suit must bid again. In other words, the bid *forces* his partner to bid again. In this case the bid is *forcing for one round*. Later on we will encounter bids that are *forcing to game*, in which it is understood that the bidding will continue until a contract sufficiently high for a game (100 points) is reached.

It might be worth reminding you here that the words 'must bid again' relate to the agreement the partners have under the system they are using, the system being put forward in this book. There is no obligation under the Laws of Bridge for anybody to bid who doesn't want to. The forcing bid is an aid players use to help them reach the best contract in the most foolproof way.

What we have been discussing is the change of suit at the One level. This switch is not possible if the suit that the responder wishes to change to is a lower-ranking suit than the suit named in the opening bid. For example, if the opening bid was 1 ♥ or 1 ♠, and the responder wished to change the suit to diamonds, he would need to bid at the Two level – 2 ♦.

To change suits at the Two level, more high-card points are required in your hand, a minimum of nine if your suit is average (four or five cards with two honours). This can be shaded down to seven or eight points if your suit is particularly strong and you feel you could rebid it after a bid by your partner. Figures 56 to 58 are examples. Changing suit at the Two level, just as at the One level, is a forcing bid for one round.

Figure 56 is a typical hand for a response of 2 ♦ over 1 ♥. Figure 57 is a hand lacking in points, but the club suit is good and if necessary you can bid it again at the Three level if your partner rebids at 2NT. Figure 58 is a

56
**Your partner has opened 1 ♥.
Your ten points and good
diamond suit are sufficient to
justify a 2 ♦ response.**

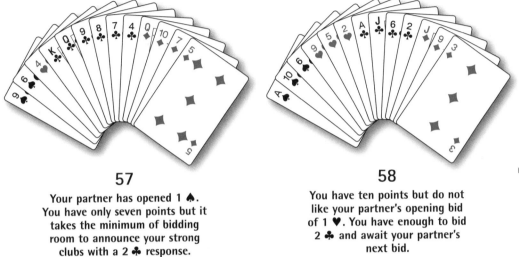

57

Your partner has opened 1 ♠. You have only seven points but it takes the minimum of bidding room to announce your strong clubs with a 2 ♣ response.

58

You have ten points but do not like your partner's opening bid of 1 ♥. You have enough to bid 2 ♣ and await your partner's next bid.

good hand for a marking-time bid. Your partner must bid again, and having told him about your clubs, you have plenty of time to find the correct contract.

Invitations to game

The fourth type of response to an opening bid of One in a suit is a strong one that suggests to your partner that there may be possibilities for a game in your two hands. It is not the strongest bid and is limited, and there are two forms. The response is either of 2NT or a *double raise* (1 ♠ to 3 ♠) in your partner's suit.

The 2NT raise is used on balanced hands of 11–13 high-card points. If

your partner has opened the bidding, he should have around 13 points at least, and if you have 11–13 then the combined hands are approaching the 25 or 26 usually taken as the requirement for making game. Figures 59 to 61 (see page 72) give examples.

Sometimes there is a tendency with a hand like that in Figure 61, where four cards to the Jack, 10 and 9 are held in your partner's suit, to make a double raise, in this case to 3 ♦. But as the hand is balanced and falls within the 11–13 point range for 2NT, perhaps 2NT is the better call. Your partner can add 11–13 points to those in his own hand and will know within three points the

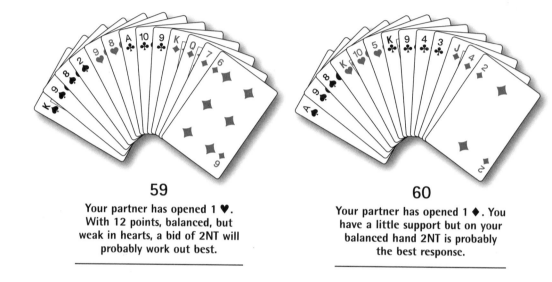

59

Your partner has opened 1 ♥.
With 12 points, balanced, but
weak in hearts, a bid of 2NT will
probably work out best.

60

Your partner has opened 1 ♦. You
have a little support but on your
balanced hand 2NT is probably
the best response.

high-card point count of the two hands
and judge his next bid accordingly. A
response of 2NT is not a forcing bid,
and if your partner's hand is a
minimum he might well feel that 2NT is
the best contract to be in.

The double raise in your partner's
suit, also called a *jump* raise, since it is
not made at the lowest possible level
but jumps one, is also an encouraging
raise. It shows good support for your
partner's suit, and is used with a hand
that has more distributional values than
that needed for 2NT. There is a promise
of about 10–12 points, but the
distribution is more important.

Nine points with four trumps and a
singleton or, if the trumps are good, a

61

You have better support than in
Figure 60 for your partner's
opening diamond bid, but again
2NT, showing a balanced 11
points, is more informative than
a response of 3 ♦.

The bidding

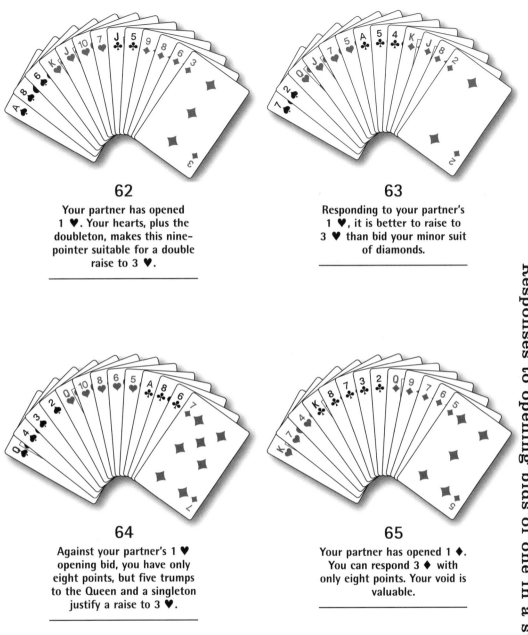

62

Your partner has opened
1 ♥. Your hearts, plus the
doubleton, makes this nine-
pointer suitable for a double
raise to 3 ♥.

63

Responding to your partner's
1 ♥, it is better to raise to
3 ♥ than bid your minor suit
of diamonds.

64

Against your partner's 1 ♥
opening bid, you have only
eight points, but five trumps
to the Queen and a singleton
justify a raise to 3 ♥.

65

Your partner has opened 1 ♦.
You can respond 3 ♦ with
only eight points. Your void is
valuable.

doubleton would suffice. If the
distribution is better still, say five trumps,
a singleton and a doubleton, then the
high-card point requirement can be

shaded down to eight. Figures 62 to 64
show hands suitable for a double raise
when responding to a bid of One in a
suit. Each time the opening bid is 1 ♥.

If your partner opens with a minor-suit bid it is usually best to respond with a bid of One in a major suit, if possible, or 2NT if you have the necessary high-card points and a balanced hand. Figure 61 shows a case of the latter, while Figure 65 shows a hand on which it would be reasonable to raise a bid of 1 ♦ to 3 ♦ despite having only eight points.

Bids direct to game

If you have an excellent fit with your partner's hand you can bid straight to game. There are two bids that would achieve this result, 3NT or a raise to the level of Four in your partner's major suit, or, rarely, to Five in a minor.

Raise to 3NT To raise to 3NT you need a balanced hand, including cards in your partner's suit, and around 14-17 points (as recommended above, with 13 points raise to 2NT). The raise to 3NT indicates the partnership has around 26 points minimum, which is enough for a game in no-trumps. Distributions suitable for a call to 3NT are shown in Figures 66 and 67.

In Figure 66 you have first-round control (Ace) or second-round (King, Queen) in all three of the suits not bid by your partner, who has opened, plus a Jack in his suit. In Figure 67, with 17 high-card points, and high values in all four suits (counting your partner's hearts), you should be safe enough in 3NT.

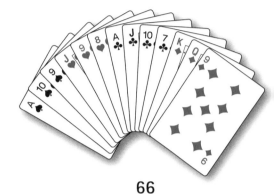

66

Over your partner's opening 1 ♥, you have a balanced 15 points, suitable for a response of 3NT.

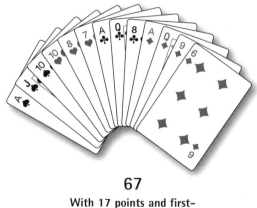

67

With 17 points and first-round control in all suits other than your partner's hearts, you can safely bid 3NT over your partner's 1 ♥.

Of course, the bidding might not end there. If your partner has bid 1 ♥ on the strength of seven hearts and a void, but is holding only 12 points, he might prefer to bid 4 ♥ and try to make game in his long suit rather than no-trumps.

Triple raise in your partner's suit   The other bid to go straight to game is to raise your partner's suit to the level of Four. For this you require at least four trumps. You will recall the high-card point count required for a double raise in partner's suit was variable, with the distribution being the most important consideration. With the triple raise, the demands in distribution are a little higher. Only 8–12 high-card points are required but voids, singletons and/or doubletons are also needed. Figures 68 and 69 show examples. Figure 68 shows a hand with five trumps and good distributional values, while Figure 69 has four strong trumps and 12 points.

It is unusual to raise direct to game in a minor suit, since that requires a big jump, but it is conceivable that on a hand like that in Figure 70 (see page 76) you might raise 1 ♦ to 4 ♦.

Jump in a new suit

With a very powerful hand where a game is virtually certain, your strongest response to an opening of One in a suit is to *jump* in a new suit. This means that you bid a new suit but not at the cheapest level you can, instead jumping

68

Your partner has opened 1 ♠. The five trumps, including the Ace, plus another Ace, a doubleton and a singleton, just justify a jump to 4 ♠.

69

You could raise your partner's 1 ♠ to 4 ♠ with this hand. At least eight trumps and 25 points should be held between you.

70

With six diamonds to the Ace,
plus ♠ A and two singletons,
you could raise 1 ♦ to 4 ♦
with this hand.

to the next level. You have combined two of the responses discussed so far – a simple change of suit *and* a double raise of your partner's suit – into one: a change of suit and a double raise. For example, if your partner opened 1 ♦, and your response is 2 ♠, you have changed suit and jumped. A simple change of suit to spades would need a bid of 1 ♠, but you have bid 2 ♠. This bid is forcing to game and neither of you should stop bidding until the level of game is reached. Of course, initially you will be wondering about a slam (see page 28), and as soon as the denomination – suit or no-trumps – is agreed, your bidding will be towards investigating a slam. Other examples of

a jump in a new suit will take you to the level of Three, for example 3 ♦ over 1 ♥, or 3 ♥ over 1 ♠.

To make a jump in a new suit you need 16 or more high-card points, which you could shave to 15 with a solid suit of your own (for example, six cards headed by Ace, King, Jack) or a good suit with very good support for your partner's suit (your intention would be to let your partner know the fit in his suit at the next stage of bidding).

Figures 71 to 73 show examples of responses with a jump in a new suit, sometimes called a jump shift.

In Figure 71, you have 16 points, the minimum recommendation to jump shift with a balanced hand, and your spades are strong enough to allow you to bid them at the Two level on this round. Since the bid is forcing to game, the bidding must continue and you have plenty of time to discover whether your spade suit or your partner's heart suit (you have some support) is the better.

In Figure 72, the hand is almost the minimum on which you can jump in a new suit. Your support for your partner's hearts is not very high, but your strong spades make it a reasonable shift.

In Figure 73, you are strongest in your partner's spade suit and have 17 high-card points. A straight jump to 3 ♠ would suggest to your partner a hand that might have no more than about 10 points, and be based on distribution, while a triple raise to 4 ♠

71

Your partner has opened 1 ♥. You have a good spade suit, some support for his hearts and 16 points. This is about the minimum for a jump to 2 ♠.

72

Your partner has opened 1 ♥. Your strong spades and control of two rounds of clubs is sufficient for a jump to 2 ♠.

73

You have 17 points and your best suit is spades, in which your partner has opened the bidding. The best option is a jump shift to 3 ♦, bidding your spades on the next round.

would suggest about 8–12 points and good distribution. In fact you are much stronger, and the solution is to jump shift to 3 ♦. Your partner must keep the bidding going at least until game is reached, and you can tell him the good news about your spades on your next chance to bid.

Opening bids of two in a suit

Sometimes hands are so strong that the simple opening bid of One in a suit, although this could cover any high-card point-holding up to about 19, seems inadequate. In terms of the requirement in points to bid 2 ♦, 2 ♥ or 2 ♠, a minimum of about 16 points is required, or 18 balanced, the top limit being 22.

At least five cards should be held in the
suit bid, which should also contain
high-card points and distribution values.
Notice that 2 ♣ is a conventional bid,
with its own special meaning, and this
will be dealt with shortly.

Opening with 2 ♦, 2 ♥ or 2 ♠

An opening bid of 2 ♦, 2 ♥ or 2 ♠ is
clearly strong, and is usually played as
a forcing bid for one round only. It
should be mentioned that some players
do not regard this bid as forcing and it
is a question for you and your partner
to decide. In the system used in this
book it is regarded as forcing.

What is the difference between an
18-point hand that is worth a bid at the
One level and one that is worth a bid at
the Two level? Your hand must be so
strong that you want to be sure of the
opportunity to bid again. You must have
at least five cards in the suit that you
bid, and be able to visualize about eight
reasonably sure winners with that suit
as trumps. In other words any sort of fit
with your partner should be enough to
give you a game. Clearly distribution is
an important factor in the choice.

Figures 74 to 78 are examples of
hands on which an opening bid at the
Two level is justified.

74

A very strong heart suit, 18 points
and eight sure tricks makes this
an obvious hand to open 2 ♥.

75

Less strong in trumps and
distribution than the hand in
Figure 74, the 21 points make this
hand worth a 2 ♥ opening bid.

76

The 21 points and strong
diamonds make this hand a
good 2 ♦ opener.

77

18 points, two good suits and a
void make this hand worth a 2 ♥
opening bid.

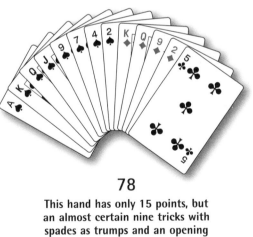

78

This hand has only 15 points, but
an almost certain nine tricks with
spades as trumps and an opening
bid of 2 ♠ is reasonable.

Opening with 2 ♣

This is our first encounter so far with a
conventional bid, otherwise known as
an *artificial bid*. It is probably the best
known and most widely used. When
you bid 2 ♣ you are revealing nothing
about your hand or strongest suit. You
are merely saying: 'I have a powerful
hand of at least 23 points, or 20 points
minimum with a strong suit and good
distribution. In other words I need very
little from my partner in order to make
game.' It is forcing to game – neither
player must pass until the bidding
reaches the level of game.

Opening with 2 ♣ ♠ ♥ ♦ ♣

Suitable hands are shown in Figures 79 to 82. With the 23-pointers in Figures 79 and 80, the partnership is only 3 points or so away from game. In each case if the opener receives a negative response from his partner (2 ♦), he should rebid 2 ♥. This allows his partner to name any long suit he might have and gives plenty of bidding space to the partnership in order to reach the best game bid.

The hand in Figure 81 contains only 20 points but has good distribution. Even with a negative response from a partner, making 4 ♥ should be comfortable, and 2 ♣ should be bid. The hand in Figure 82 is the opposite – no long suit but the point count of 26 needs only one or two useful cards from your partner to make a game certain.

Responses to opening bids of two in a suit

If your partner opens with 2 ♦, 2 ♥ or 2 ♠, you must respond for at least one round. If your hand has six points or fewer give a negative response – 2NT. By adding six points to those in his hand, the opener has an upper limit for the points held by the two hands together. It will probably not be enough for a game, and the likelihood is that your partner will repeat his suit at the Three level. This is not forcing, and the bidding might end there.

However, if your partner introduces a new suit, such as in a sequence like

79
This hand of 23 points should be opened 2 ♣.

80
Another ideal hand for a 2 ♣ opening bid.

81

A hand with only 20 points but, with the void, first-round control in every suit. Although the final contract will probably be in hearts, a bid of 2 ♣ is not unreasonable.

2 ♥, 2NT then 3 ♣, the rebid is again forcing for one round. In the example, the response should be 4 ♣ if the responder has four or five cards in the suit, otherwise he should bid the original opening suit – 3 ♥.

If the responder holds seven or more points opposite his partner's opening bid at the Two level, he can either raise his partner's suit or introduce a strong suit of his own. As the opener will have at least five good cards in his suit for the Two bid, three cards in support, including an honour, is regarded as sufficient for the single raise. Figure 83 shows a hand that suits this raise.

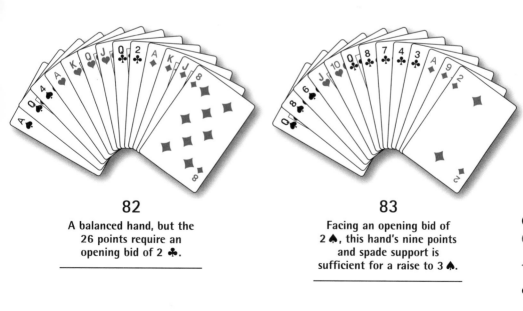

82

A balanced hand, but the 26 points require an opening bid of 2 ♣.

83

Facing an opening bid of 2 ♠, this hand's nine points and spade support is sufficient for a raise to 3 ♠.

♠
♥
♦
♣

On the other hand, if the responder holds the hand shown in Figure 84, he can bid 3 ♦. This tells his partner that he has at least seven points and a good diamond suit. He will probably bid on to game or even a slam.

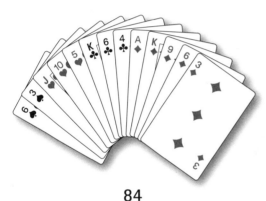

84

Your partner has opened 2 ♠. The 11 points and good diamond suit justify a response of 3 ♦.

Responses to a bid of 2 ♣

The negative response to a bid of 2 ♣ is 2 ♦. This tells your partner that you have six points or fewer. Any other response is positive and shows seven or more points, in which case bid Two in your best suit, which would be your longest. Since with his 2 ♣ bid the opener has not yet named a suit, he will then go on to bid his suit.

With a balanced hand you can respond to an opening 2 ♣ with 2NT. This bid does not imply weakness, as it does after an opening of Two in a suit other than clubs.

If you hold the hand in Figure 85, you should bid 2 ♥, telling your partner of your good heart suit.

85

With nine points over your partner's opening bid of 2 ♣, you bid your longest suit, 2 ♥.

Figure 86 shows a 10-pointer with strong diamonds. A response of 2 ♦ would be negative, but your hand is strong enough to respond 3 ♦.

Opening bids of three or more in a suit

We meet a new concept when considering opening bids at the level of Three or Four in a suit. They are not strong bids at all – certainly not stronger than an opening bid at the Two level.

An opening bid of Three or Four is called a *pre-emptive* bid (or pre-empt). According to the dictionary, the word is used mostly in Bridge and in warfare, and means, basically, 'getting in first'.

A pre-emptive strike in war hits the enemy before he has the chance of hitting you, and in Bridge a pre-emptive bid is designed to take the bidding high before the opposition has a chance to get their bidding going. The assumption of the bidder is that the opposition players probably have the stronger hands and the bid is to hinder them while not placing his own side in too much danger.

Consider the hand in Figure 87. You are the dealer, so nobody has yet bid. You have three points fewer than average but with diamonds as trumps would expect to make about six tricks from your own hand. Consider the implications. If you bid 3 ♦ and your

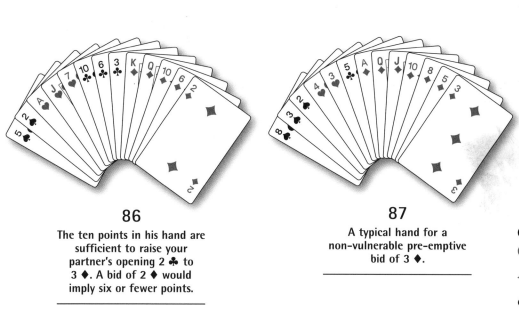

86
The ten points in his hand are sufficient to raise your partner's opening 2 ♣ to 3 ♦. A bid of 2 ♦ would imply six or fewer points.

87
A typical hand for a non-vulnerable pre-emptive bid of 3 ♦.

partner can contribute three tricks, you will make your contract for a part-score. Suppose your partner has a really bad hand (say three points) and doesn't help at all, and you go down by three tricks and are doubled. The penalty is 500 points – quite substantial. It will be reduced by the fact that with four honours you can claim 100 points – so your deficit is 400. However, if you and your partner have only 10 points between you, your opponents must have 30. They have missed at least a game, possibly a slam.

So your loss of 400 points is not a bad outcome given the hands as they were dealt. Often, of course, your pre-emptive bid will not stand, and your opponents will outbid you. But after your 3 ♦, the lowest bid they can start at is 3 ♥.

They could easily, in the bidding space allowed them, go wrong. Your bid has made it more difficult for them to find the right contract for themselves.

However, there are other things to consider with the pre-emptive bid. The first concerns vulnerability. You will remember from the scoring section that when you are vulnerable the penalties for failure to make a contract are more severe. In the example mentioned, where three down cost 500 points, the penalty had you been vulnerable would have been 800, which is more than the bonus for winning a rubber. So you must be more cautious in making this

bid if you are vulnerable. As a guide, if you are not vulnerable you must be reasonably sure of making six tricks; if you are vulnerable this requirement rises to seven tricks. So, if you are vulnerable, you would pass with the hand in Figure 87.

The other consideration in making a pre-emptive bid is your position at the table. Pre-emptive bids are made on the first round of bidding. As dealer, not vulnerable, you could pre-empt with the hand in Figure 88. As third caller, after two passes, you would do the same. As second caller, however, after a pass by the dealer, you might prefer to pass, since the likelihood of your partner having a good hand has

88

As first or third caller, not vulnerable, you could pre-empt with 3 ♦ on this hand, but in second or fourth positions might pass.

The bidding ♠ ♥ ♦ ♣

increased. If he bids, you can respond with your diamonds on the next round. In the fourth position, too, your better option is to pass and hope for more than seven points in the next deal. You can pre-empt in second position if the dealer has opened the bidding. After an opening bid at the level of One, and holding the hand in Figure 88, you should bid 3 ♦.

This means that the dealer's partner has to respond at the Three level and denies your opponents bidding space.

The pre-emptive bid is made when your hand is not suitable for an opening bid of One, so it is typically made with 6–10 high-card points. It requires a strong suit of seven or more cards, headed by three or four honours. It should be made if your hand has practically no strength in defence at all (the hands in Figures 87 and 88 could not be relied upon for more than one trick in defence). If you are not vulnerable, you should be able to count on six playing tricks – that is, tricks you are almost certain to win. If you are vulnerable, this requirement goes up to seven tricks.

Pre-empting is a defensive form of bidding. You know, or suspect, that the opposition has the balance of high-card points. You will not be surprised after a pre-emptive bid either to be outbid by your opponents, or to fail to make your contract. You are, in a way, at least limiting the damage.

Opening bids of four or five in a suit

Opening with Four in a suit is also pre-emptive. In fact, the same principles apply as to opening Three in a suit. You just need to be a little stronger. Consider the hand in Figure 89. You can count on a possible seven or eight tricks – seven almost for sure, with the eighth trump probably providing another. If you are vulnerable open with 3 ♥, but if not vulnerable open with 4 ♥.

A simple way of deciding how many to pre-empt is to count your playing tricks, adding three if not vulnerable, two if vulnerable, and bid to make that number of tricks. If the answer is nine, pre-empt at the Three level. If the answer is fewer than nine, pass.

89
A hand with which you might open 4 ♥.

With eight or nine playing tricks of your own, pre-empt at the Four level at any vulnerability, and if your suit is a minor suit, open at the Five level. Figure 90 is an example of a hand on which you might open 5 ♦.

Responses to opening bids of three or more in a suit

The first thing to realize when responding to a pre-emptive bid of Three in a suit is that your partner is weak, and holds practically nothing outside the suit he bid. It is likely that you will be very weak in that suit (after all, he might hold eight of the cards in the suit). However, you might be very strong in another suit yourself, and be tempted to bid the suit. Beware! Do not try to 'rescue' your partner from a pre-empt, or to fight him over the suit. Only do it with a long, exceptionally powerful suit of your own, as in Figure 91. A change of suit in response to a pre-emptive bid is forcing.

The main consideration when responding to a pre-emptive bid with a good hand yourself is whether to raise to game in your partner's suit. As stated earlier, your partner should be able to count on six playing tricks if not vulnerable, and seven if vulnerable, when making his pre-emptive bid. To raise to game, then, you should be able to provide four tricks if not vulnerable and three if vulnerable. In making this calculation you should count the Ace,

90
With this hand, you have nine playing tricks with diamonds as trumps. You could make a pre-emptive opening bid of 5 ♦.

91
Your partner has pre-empted with 3 ♥. With 16 points, your spade suit is strong enough to bid 3 ♠, a forcing bid.

King or Queen of your partner's suit as one trick each. In other suits (known as *outside* suits) count an Ace and King as two tricks; an Ace and Queen as one and a half; an Ace as one; and a King and Queen as one. If you have three or more cards in your partner's suit, you can count a void as two tricks and a singleton as one. Add the total tricks thus calculated to your partner's six (not vulnerable) or seven (vulnerable) and if the total comes to enough tricks for game, you can raise to game. If not, do not be tempted.

Figures 92 and 93 show examples of hands on which you might consider raising 3 ♥ to 4 ♥. In Figure 92, you have three hearts to the King, and a singleton club, which should produce two tricks, and the ♠ A and Q, which should produce either one or two. With three and a half playing tricks, you can raise to game if vulnerable, since your partner should be confident of seven tricks from his hand. However, it would be a risk to raise to 4 ♥ if not vulnerable, bearing in mind the opponents could well hold 22 or 23 high-card points. In Figure 93 you hold a much stronger hand at first glance, with 13 points including two Aces, but those Aces might be the only tricks the hand makes, and the hand is not strong enough to raise to 4 ♥.

You might hold a hand that justifies a raise of a pre-emptive bid to game by bidding 3NT. Such a hand must have

92

Your partner has bid 3 ♥. This hand has three and a half playing tricks (one for ♥ K, one for singleton, one and a half for ♠ A and Q). Raise to 4 ♥ if vulnerable, but not if not vulnerable.

93

Your partner has bid 3 ♥. Although you have 13 points, you can count only two and a half playing tricks, not enough to raise to game.

good guards (explained shortly) in the three unbid suits and preferably three cards in your partner's suit, since you might need to enter (see page 129) his hand twice to *clear the suit* (eliminate it from the other three hands so that each remaining card in the suit is a winner). Such a hand is shown in Figure 94.

A bid of 3NT in this situation should be understood by you and your partner as a contract you want to play in, so your partner need not bid on. It is what is known as a *signing-off bid*.

Figure 95 shows a different hand altogether. You have a 2 ♣ opening bid yourself. The only thing that can stop you making 7NT is if your partner pre-empts with seven hearts missing the Ace and Queen (you hold the King). If he holds the ♥ A, you will make all the tricks. You can find out if he has the ♥ A by bidding 4NT, which is an artificial bid. We will explain how that bid works shortly (see page 111).

Responses to a pre-empt of four or five in a suit

Basically the same principles of responding to a pre-emptive bid at the Three level apply to the responses at the level of Four or Five. Of course, if your partner has pre-empted with 4 ♥ or 4 ♠, there is no point in raising him as the bid is already worth game, unless

94

Over your partner's 3 ♥ pre-empt, you could raise to 3NT, the vital requirement being enough hearts to establish and enter your partner's long suit.

95

Your partner has opened 3 ♥. If his hearts are seven to the Ace, or six to the Ace and Queen, you will make 13 tricks. Bid 4NT (see page 111).

your hand is so strong that a slam becomes a possibility. You can then bid 4NT as with the example in Figure 95, if you wish to be sure he has the Ace of his suit.

Responses to a pre-empt: summary

The main thing to remember when responding to a pre-empt is that your partner is weak, so the fact that you might hold an above-average hand is not surprising. While there might be a game or even a slam on, do not rush into anything. Remember that nine times out of ten the best policy is to pass and let your partner attempt to make the contract. So weigh up the possibilities carefully before bidding on.

Opening the bidding in no-trumps

Opening the bidding with a bid of no-trumps is largely a question of how many high-card points you hold in your hand. One of the questions that a partnership has to decide when working out its bidding system is whether to play what is called a 'strong no-trump' or a 'weak no-trump' (see panel). In this book we advocate a strong no-trump, in which an opening bid of 1NT promises your partner that you hold 16–18 high-card points.

WEAK AND STRONG NO-TRUMPS

● ●

In the original Acol system (see page 56), an opening of 1NT when not vulnerable indicated a hand with 13–15 points. This is called a 'weak no-trump'. When vulnerable, the range was 16–18 points. This is a 'strong no-trump'. Over the years the practice became for the weak no-trump to indicate 12–14 points. Many players decided to use the weak no-trump or the strong no-trump exclusively, whatever the vulnerability. Sometimes, players who use only the strong no-trump amend the points requirement to 15–17. This book advocates the use of a strong no-trump, requiring 16–18 points, at all times.

Opening 1NT

The high-card count requirement to open the bidding at 1NT is, as already mentioned, 16–18. The hand should be balanced – that is, of the patterns 4-3-3-3, 4-4-3-2 or 5-3-3-2. You need a *guard* or a near-guard in every suit. A guard is a card that prevents an opponent from running a long suit and picking up several tricks. For example, an Ace is the best guard, because if its suit is led it can win the trick immediately if its holder wishes. A King and Queen combination is the next best, because it ensures control of the suit once the Ace is played – in other words an opponent with a long suit headed by the Ace can make only the Ace in that suit before giving you the lead. A King with another card or two is a near-guard, but not a complete one. It will win the second trick in its suit, if the Ace is led first. In a hand of the 5-3-3-2 type, the doubleton must have one high card at least to justify a no-trump opening – a doubleton of two small cards is worthless.

Figures 96 to 98 show hands suitable for opening 1NT. That in Figure 98 is one point short, but you can cheat a little with the good intermediate strength – three 10s, a 9 and two 8s. Similarly, a hand of 19 points, one point over the limit, but with no intermediates, could be opened 1NT. While not being a slave to the point count, do not stray more than one point either way, as it would mislead

96
A perfect hand for opening 1NT: 18 points and balanced.

97
A balanced hand of 17 points: open 1NT.

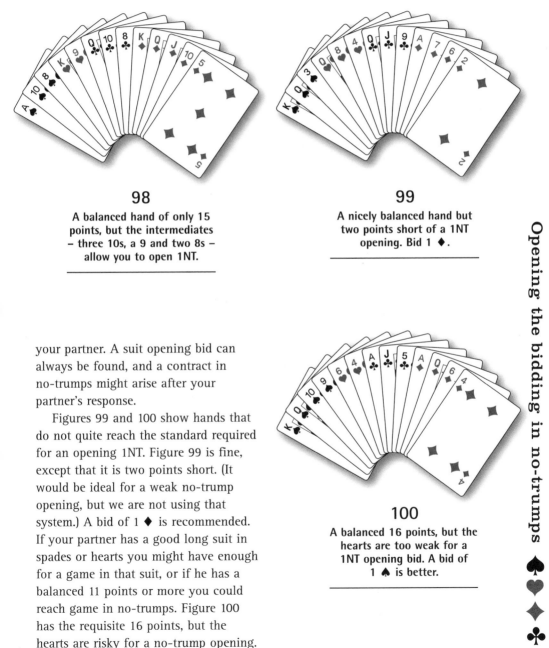

98

A balanced hand of only 15
points, but the intermediates
– three 10s, a 9 and two 8s –
allow you to open 1NT.

99

A nicely balanced hand but
two points short of a 1NT
opening. Bid 1 ♦.

your partner. A suit opening bid can
always be found, and a contract in
no-trumps might arise after your
partner's response.

Figures 99 and 100 show hands that
do not quite reach the standard required
for an opening 1NT. Figure 99 is fine,
except that it is two points short. (It
would be ideal for a weak no-trump
opening, but we are not using that
system.) A bid of 1 ♦ is recommended.
If your partner has a good long suit in
spades or hearts you might have enough
for a game in that suit, or if he has a
balanced 11 points or more you could
reach game in no-trumps. Figure 100
has the requisite 16 points, but the
hearts are risky for a no-trump opening.

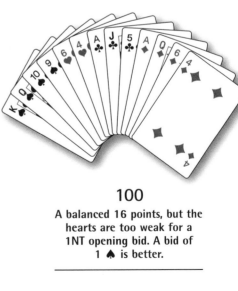

100

A balanced 16 points, but the
hearts are too weak for a
1NT opening bid. A bid of
1 ♠ is better.

If your partner has good hearts, you could still end in a no-trump contract.

Opening 2NT

To open with a bid of 2NT, much the same principles apply as those needed for 1NT, except that the hand has to be about four high-card points stronger (20–22). There is perhaps an even stronger requirement for the hand to be balanced, and any suit that doesn't contain a card as high as Queen ought to have length (four cards). Intermediate values should be taken into account. Figures 101 and 102 show hands suitable for a 2NT opening.

Just as it is possible to stretch the lower limit of the points requirement to 19 for a 2NT opening, it is possible to open 2NT with a 23-point hand, recommended earlier for a 2 ♣ opening bid. If the 23-pointer is balanced, without being really powerful in any suit – a bits-and-pieces hand – it is reasonable to open 2NT rather than 2 ♣. Figure 103 shows such a hand, where the choice is almost an even one.

Be particularly aware of weak suits when considering making a 2NT opening. Figure 104 shows a hand with a weak diamond suit. An approach bid (one that feels out your partner's strengths) of 1 ♣ might be best. A positive response from partner should lead to a game somewhere.

A bid of 2NT is not absolutely forcing, since your partner can pass if

101

A balanced 22-point hand, suitable for a bid of 2NT.

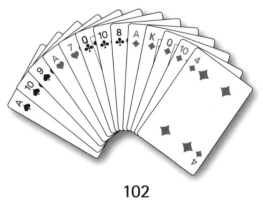

102

Only 19 points, but the strong diamond suit and good intermediates make it suitable for a 2NT bid.

103

The 23 points of this hand qualify it for a 2 ♣ opening bid but it is balanced and lacks a very powerful suit and is better opened 2NT.

he holds fewer than four high-card points. With five points or more the combined hands are obviously in the range for making game and your partner will respond.

Opening 3NT

An opening bid of 3NT is not often used and is probably best avoided by beginners. It is something of a gamble. In the Acol system it is made with a hand that contains a long solid minor suit and high cards in at least two other suits. Figure 105 is an example, showing a hand from which, as soon as the holder gets the lead with either ♠ A

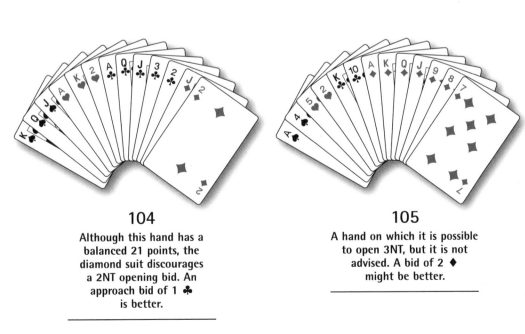

104

Although this hand has a balanced 21 points, the diamond suit discourages a 2NT opening bid. An approach bid of 1 ♣ is better.

105

A hand on which it is possible to open 3NT, but it is not advised. A bid of 2 ♦ might be better.

or ♣ K, will probably make seven tricks in diamonds. It relies on the opponents being unable to win several tricks in hearts or clubs before you can cash your diamonds.

Many players prefer not to use this convention. If it is not being used, 3NT might be opened on a balanced hand with 23–25 points, but opening 2 ♣, as described in the first section, is probably a better convention to use with such a hand.

Responses to opening bids in no-trumps

Responses to no-trump opening bids are in one sense reasonably straightforward, because the responder knows, to within a point or three, the high-card count of the opener's hand, and also that it is of a balanced shape.

Responses to an opening bid of 1NT

The responder can calculate quickly the chances of game, since he knows his partner has in the region of 16–18 points. Let us assume first that the responder has a balanced hand. To succeed in making a game of 3NT it is generally recognized that a combined total of 25 points is required. It follows that with seven points or more, the responder can see possibilities of making a game, and should bid. However, with six points or fewer, making game is doubtful. There is no point in bidding higher but stopping before game – you

are merely increasing the chances of failing to make your contract. So if you have a balanced hand and six points or fewer, pass.

With 7 or 8 points and a balanced hand, the combined count would be 23–26, depending upon whether your partner opened with a minimum 16 or a maximum 18. The response then is 2NT. This tells your partner that if his opening bid was at the strong end of the range, he can raise to 3NT. If not, then he can leave the level at 2NT.

If the responder has a balanced hand of 9 points or more, then he knows that the combined point count is at least 25, and chances of making game in 3NT are good, so he could bid straight to 3NT, which his partner will see as a sign-off.

If your hand contains a singleton or a void plus a reasonable suit of five cards or more, it is generally better to respond in a suit rather than in no-trumps. You do not need more than five points to switch to a suit, but with four or fewer, however unbalanced, you should pass. With five or more switch to Two of your longest suit, unless that suit is clubs. A raise to 2 ♣ is another conventional bid, as we will soon see. A raise to 2 ♦, 2 ♥ or 2 ♠ tells your partner that you are weak, specifically with 5–7 points, but that you have at least five cards of the suit you have named. Unless that suit happens to be the opener's weakest, he will probably let the bidding end there – otherwise he will switch back to 2NT, where you should leave him.

Figure 106 shows a hand on which you can raise a bid of 1NT to a suit bid at the level of Two (a single raise on 1NT). If your partner has four diamonds or three good ones, he might leave the contract there. If not, you should respect his decision.

If you hold eight points or more in an unbalanced hand, with a good major suit of at least five cards, you can make an invitation to game with a double raise in that suit. This is a forcing bid and invites your partner to raise to four in your suit or sign off in 3NT. Figure 107 shows such a hand. The combined count is 25–27 points. The opener now has to choose whether to agree to your suit and bid 4 ♥, which he should do if his hearts are strong, or to switch back to 3NT, which he should do if his hearts were weaker, say a doubleton.

If you hold nine points or more in an unbalanced hand with a long minor suit, it is probably best to bid straight to game at 3NT, rather than naming your minor suit, because to make game in a minor suit requires making 11 tricks. With the stronger hand balanced, it is usually better to settle for making only nine tricks in no-trumps. Figure 108 (see page 96) shows such a hand. This hand has the ♣ Q and 10, rather than ♥ Q and 10, making clubs a strong six-card suit. However, a contract of 5 ♣ is far from certain

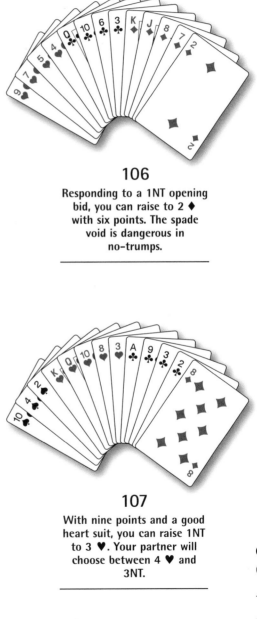

106

Responding to a 1NT opening bid, you can raise to 2 ♦ with six points. The spade void is dangerous in no-trumps.

107

With nine points and a good heart suit, you can raise 1NT to 3 ♥. Your partner will choose between 4 ♥ and 3NT.

108

With two hearts from Figure 107 switched to clubs, it is better to respond 3NT on this hand, probably easier to make than 5 ♣.

with this hand, even facing a balanced 18-pointer, and a bid of 3NT is advised.

Sometimes the responder will hold a hand of nine points or more, but with a weak suit which discourages him from trying for a no-trump game. However, he holds a good major suit of four cards which, with a combined point count of 25–27 in the two hands, would make a game contract in his major suit a good proposition if only his partner held four cards in that suit, making eight trumps between the two hands. He cannot double raise to three in his suit, since that promises five cards in the suit.

The answer is to use the *Stayman convention*. The responder makes the artificial bid of 2 ♣. This requires his partner to bid 2 ♠ if he holds four spades and 2 ♥ if he holds four hearts. If he does not hold four in either suit he will bid 2 ♦.

Should the responder discover that he and his partner hold four cards in the same major he can bid four of the suit. If he gets a 2 ♦ negative response he can revert to 2NT.

Figure 109 shows a responder's hand strong in both majors. He should respond 2 ♣. If the opener rebids 2 ♥ or 2 ♠, he can raise to Four. If the opener rebids 2 ♦, denying a four-card major suit, the responder can bid 3NT, knowing that he and his partner have a minimum of 26 points between them. If the responder has only nine points, as in Figure 110, he can bid 2 ♣ to ask if

109

Against an opening 1NT, respond 2 ♣, the Stayman convention, asking your partner if he holds four cards in spades or hearts.

110

Against an opening 1NT, investigate the possibility of a game in spades with a bid of 2 ♣ (Stayman).

the opener has four spades. If his partner does not bid 2 ♠, the responder could bid 2NT and allow his partner to raise to 3NT should he have a maximum 18 for his opening bid, which would give the pair 27 points.

Responses to an opening bid of 2NT

With a balanced hand you require only five points to raise partner to 3NT, as your combined count will be at least 25 points. You can reduce this to four points if you have good intermediates. With fewer than four points, pass and let partner play in 2NT.

A bid of Three in a suit is forcing, though it does not show a strong hand – you can bid a major suit if you have at least five cards in it and as few as five points. Figure 111 (see page 98) shows a hand in point. You have seven points, meaning that you and partner should hold 27–29, enough for a game. As the bid is forcing, partner cannot pass, and with the knowledge that you hold five spades will choose between raises to 4 ♠ or 3NT according to his own hand.

It is not advisable raising to the Three level in a suit if it is a minor suit of five cards, even with six or seven points. Figure 112 shows one such hand. You could make a long diamond or two in no-trumps, and will need to make two fewer tricks for game in 3NT than 5 ♦.

If, facing a partner who has opened 2NT, you hold 12 points or more, you

THE STAYMAN CONVENTION

· · · · · · · · · · · · · · · · · · · ·

The response of 2 ♣ to a 1NT opener as a request to bid a four-card major suit arose in the early 1930s in a slightly different form, which in 1945 was adapted in the US by George Rapee and used by him and his partner Sam Stayman. It was used in England about the same time by J.C.H. Marx. All three were prominent players and writers. Simon 'Skid' Skidelsky, who wrote novels and humorous Bridge-books under the name S.J. Simon, and who was, with Marx, one of the devisers of the Acol system, suggested the 2 ♦ negative response, and this became generally adopted. The convention was extensively publicized in the 1950s by Stayman, who with Rapee was a world champion three times in that decade, and it became one of the most widely used bidding conventions.

111

Your partner has opened 2NT. Your seven points and five spades are sufficient to bid 3 ♠, which is forcing. Your partner must choose between 3NT and 4 ♠.

112

Despite holding five diamonds to the Ace, and six points, it is not worth responding 3 ♦ on this hand to a 2NT opening bid. Bid 3NT, which is easier to make than a game in diamonds.

might well be in small slam range; 16 points and a grand slam is possible. We will discuss these situations in a later section, where we reach the later stages of bidding.

Responses to an opening bid of 3NT

We recommend beginners avoid opening 3NT, but if you decide to use it conventionally, with your partner opening 3NT with a solid minor suit and high cards in at least two others, then as responder you should pass, unless your hand contains something like three Aces and a King. This suggests you might have the makings of a slam. In this case you should bid your longest suit at the Four level.

Your partner can bid 4NT, a convention (Blackwood) that we will come to on page 111. It enables your partner to discover how many Aces you have and from that he can work out his final bid, which you should respect.

Rebids after opening with one of a suit

Having looked at various opening bids, and the responses that can be made to them, we now come to the continuation, or the second round and beyond. How does the opening bidder respond to the responder? The second bid of the opening bidder is called a *rebid*. In this section we look at rebids after various responses to a suit bid at the One level – 1 ♣, 1 ♦, 1 ♥ and 1 ♠.

EASLEY BLACKWOOD

● ●

Easley Blackwood was born in 1903 and invented the Blackwood four no-trump artificial convention in 1933 (see page 111).
An insurance manager, he was one of the most famous Bridge personalities and writers of his day, writing several books, articles and newspaper columns. His convention remains one of the most widely used in Bridge.

Rebid after a 1NT response

A response of 1NT is made when the opener has bid One of a suit. This particular response shows 6–9 points, no great support for the opener's suit and no very strong suit at all. If, as rebidder, you have a balanced hand, you can think of progressing in no-trumps. With 19 points of your own (making 25–28 in the combined hands), you can raise to 3NT. Your partner will pass. With a little fewer, 17 points, you can raise to 2NT. Again, your partner should pass.

If your suit is strong, and you have 15 points, you can make a jump rebid

♠
♥
♦
♣

in your suit, say from 1 ♠ to 3 ♠. This tells your partner your situation. If he is at the top end of his range, at nine points, he can re-evaluate his hand in light of your good suit and work out if 4 ♠ or 3NT might be a reasonable proposition. If so, he can raise to whichever game is more attractive, and pass if he thinks 3 ♠ is maximum. Such a bidding situation is shown in Figure 113. In this case East can bid 4 ♠, which has a good chance of succeeding.

If the opener has a strong second suit (he began with two suits of five cards say) he could bid his second suit. He should do this at the minimum level if he has fewer than 16 points, jumping to the level of Three if he has 16 or more. Once again his partner can re-evaluate his hand in the light of what this tells him and pass or bid on as he sees fit.

After a 1NT response, a jump in a second suit is forcing, and could be made with a very strong two-suiter, allowing his partner to show support for the second suit if he has it.

Should the opener himself have something not much more than a minimum opening hand and gets the response of 1NT, he can either leave it at that or rebid his suit at the Two level, where his partner should leave him.

Rebids after a 2NT response
A response of 2NT to an opening bid of a suit at One level shows 11–13 high-card points and a balanced hand.

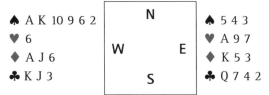

♠ A K 10 9 6 2
♥ 6
♦ A J 6
♣ K J 3

♠ 5 4 3
♥ A 9 7
♦ K 5 3
♣ Q 7 4 2

113
West deals and without opposition the bidding goes 1 ♠, 1NT and 3 ♠. East can now decide if 3NT or 4 ♠ can be made. In this case the best bid is 4 ♠.

Except after a very weak opening bid, the rebidder should bid straight to game in his suit, as he can rely on at least 11 points to add to his own count, which should put him into the range for a game. If he made a weakish opening, he should raise his suit to the Three level, warning his partner that his opening bid was based on an unbalanced distribution and that it is minimum so far as high-card points are concerned. The responder should regard this as a sign-off, and should not bid further.

If the rebidder holds a powerful two-suiter of the type shown in Figure 114 he can bid his second suit at the Three level. This is forcing and alerts his partner to the possibility of a slam. Having opened 1 ♠ and received a 2NT response, the holder of the hand in

114

On this two-suiter, the opener has bid 1 ♠. Opposite a response of 2NT he can rebid 3 ♣ (see Figure 115).

115

This is the hand opposite that in Figure 114. The bidding has gone 1 ♠, 2NT and 3 ♣ (forcing). Looking at the hands together it can be seen that a grand slam is on.

Figure 114 can bid 3 ♣. He knows the responder has 11–13 points, and if these include the ♥ A and ♣ A and four cards in spades or clubs, a slam is a possibility. Suppose, for instance, the responder holds the hand in Figure 115. A slam is a certainty, and the partnership should reach at least a small slam, with the help of another convention, the *Blackwood convention*, which will be described later, with reference to this example.

When the rebidder names a second suit, after a response of 2NT, the responder has three choices: to support the second suit (in the case of the hand in Figure 115 by bidding 4 ♣), to show preference for the first suit (by bidding 3 ♠) or to deny any interest in either by bidding 3NT, which the rebidder should accept as a sign-off bid. In the example (Figures 114 and 115) the response to the rebid would be 4 ♣ and ultimately a slam should be bid.

Rebids after a single raise response

The single raise in the opener's suit is a limited response, showing 6–9 points with some support for the bid suit, such as four small cards or three to a Queen. Unless you hold about 17 points, a game in no-trumps is unlikely unless you hold a suit that your partner's support should make fairly solid as well as guards in the other three suits. Figure 116 (see page 102) shows such a hand. Three diamonds to the Queen, or four

♠
♥
♦
♣

smaller ones, would make the diamond suit good enough for six or seven tricks in no-trumps. You can rebid 2NT. If your partner can contribute to a guard in the other three suits, he can bid 3NT, otherwise he should bid 3 ♦, which should be left, as the prospect of game in diamonds is remote. Figure 117 shows the sort of hand the responder might have. The two hands together should make 3NT without problems, and this should be the responder's final bid.

If you hold 19 points when your partner raises your suit, you have at least 25–28 points between you and trumps in both hands, so can bid straight to game in your suit.

With 14 points or fewer in your hand you are unlikely to make game, as your combined point count will probably not exceed 23, and it is best to leave the bid in Two of your suit.

It is the 15–18 range that is most awkward. The change of suit, which is forcing for one round, is a way to keep the bidding going in search of a fit that might make game. Suppose you held the hand in Figure 118. By bidding 3 ♣ you are asking your partner to bid again. You are not asking him about the possibility of a game in clubs, since you have already agreed on hearts. You are telling him that clubs is your second suit, and that if he has a fit in clubs as well as hearts and his raise was at the higher end of the scale, eight or nine points, then game might be on. He can

116

Having opened 1 ♦ you receive a response of 2 ♦. You should bid 2NT, inviting your partner to raise to 3NT if suitable, or revert to 3 ♦ (see Figure 117).

117

You are the responder and the bidding has gone 1 ♦, 2 ♦ and 2NT (see Figure 116). With guards in the other three suits, bid 3NT.

118
You have opened 1 ♥ (16 points) and your partner has responded 2 ♥. Making game is a possibility if your partner has support in clubs, too. Bid 3 ♣ (forcing).

119
This could be the responder's hand facing that in Figure 118. After 1 ♥, 2 ♥ and 3 ♣, bid 4 ♥. Game should be on (despite a combined count of only 24 points).

reassess his hand. If he has a void or singleton in spades or diamonds that would improve his hand. With a good supporting hand he can bid straight to 4 ♥, otherwise he should bid 3 ♥, which you regard as a sign-off. Figure 119 shows a hand where he could bid to 4 ♥, which should be made.

Rebids after a double raise response
When your partner raises your opening bid from One to Three he has good support for your suit, say four cards to an honour, and either around 9–12 points or good distribution, perhaps a void or a singleton. It is an invitation to bid to game. If your suit is a major suit, you should bid straight to game, e.g. 1 ♥ - 3 ♥ - 4 ♥, unless you have only a minimum opening hand yourself.

If your suit is a minor suit, and your hand balanced, you might try bidding 3NT, leaving your partner to decide whether to try for game or bid 4 ♦. If he has 12 points and high cards in the outside suits, he can bid 3NT, but if he has a singleton or a weak suit he should shift back to diamonds. There is probably not a game to be made.

Rebids after a shift at the one level
If your partner changes suit (and has not passed originally) he is saying he has a good suit of his own, but cannot support yours. His strength in high-card points could range from 5–18 or so, so you have no indication of his hand's

♠
♥
♦
♣

strength. It could be stronger than yours, and he might have game in mind himself. Therefore this bid is forcing. You cannot pass. Your rebid should convey information to your partner, and can be considered at four levels.

(a) Minimum rebids that limit your hand

These rebids tell your partner that your opening bid was little more than minimum – 15 points or fewer. These bids can be a rebid of 1NT, a raise of your partner's suit at the lowest level, or a rebid of your own suit at the lowest level. Figures 120 to 122 show examples of each. In each you have bid 1 ♦ and your partner responded 1 ♥.

In Figure 120 you have 14 points and a balanced hand. You can take into account the fact that your partner has hearts. Bid 1NT. Your heart suit is not strong enough to encourage your partner in his own suit. With this bid, you have given him a pretty good idea of your hand, and he can base his further bidding on this.

Figure 121 shows a single raise of your partner's suit. With this hand it is a nice choice of which limit bid you make, but your support for his suit is probably the most useful information you can give partner.

Figure 122 shows a hand where your limit bid should be a repeat of your own suit. Your diamond suit is strong. To bid hearts would deceive your partner and you are not balanced enough for 1NT.

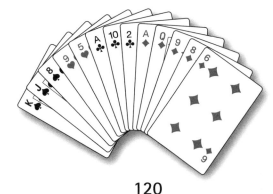

120

After a response of 1 ♥ to your 1 ♦, you can bid 1NT, limiting your hand to 15 points (you have 14) and indicating that you hold spade and club guards.

121

Again after 1 ♦ and 1 ♥, you should give a limited response (14 points). Your best bid is 2 ♥ showing a little support for your partner's suit.

The bidding

♠
♥
♦
♣

104

122

Again after 1 ♦ and 1 ♥, you must limit your rebid (14 points). A rebid of your only suit – 2 ♦ – is best.

(b) Rebidding a Third Suit at the Lowest Level You can rebid a third suit at the lowest level if you have at least four cards in that suit. The points range is from a minimum opening bid (around 13) to 18. Introducing a third suit at the lowest level involves sequences like the following:

(a) 1 ♣ – 1 ♥ – 1 ♠
(b) 1 ♦ – 1 ♠ – 2 ♣
(c) 1 ♥ – 1 ♠ – 2 ♦

However, be aware of the *reverse bid.* This is a bid at the Two level, in a higher-ranking suit than that which you bid at the One level. For example, sequences like:

(a) 1 ♦ – 1 ♠ – 2 ♥
(b) 1 ♣ – 1 ♥ – 2 ♦

In these cases the third bid introduces a third suit at the lowest level possible, but it has the drawback that if your partner wants to show preference for your first suit rather than your second, he must now bid at the Three level: 3 ♦ in the first example and 3 ♣ in the second.

To introduce a third suit by means of a reverse bid requires more strength, 17 or more points. It also guarantees at least five cards in the first suit. Figures 123 and 124 (see page 106) show hands suitable for rebidding a third suit.

In Figure 123 you have 15 points, enough to bid 2 ♦ – a new suit – over your opening 1 ♥ and your partner's response of 1 ♠. Figure 124 shows a reverse bid. The hearts and diamonds of Figure 123 have been switched, so that your opening bid would be 1 ♦. Again your partner responds 1 ♠. Had the spades and clubs remained the same as in Figure 123, a rebid of 2 ♥ would be debatable with 15 points. But with Ace instead of Queen of clubs, making 17 points, as in the example, 2 ♥, a reverse bid, is the best rebid.

(c) A Jump Rebid to Show a Strong Hand
Your partner has responded by naming his suit at the One level over your opening bid. This promises little except that he has at least five points and a good suit. If your hand is better than a

♠
♥
♦
♣

123

You have opened 1 ♥ and the response is 1 ♠. Your 15 points and good diamonds justify a rebid of 2 ♦.

minimum, containing 16 points or more, you can show this in three ways other than the reverse bid mentioned above. These are by bidding 2NT, by a jump rebid in your own suit, or by a double raise of your partner's suit.

A rebid of 2NT is made with a balanced 16–18 points. Figure 125 shows such a hand. If your partner has nine points or more he can raise to 3NT.

A jump rebid in your own suit is made when that suit is exceptionally strong, preferably with at least six cards. Figure 126 shows such a hand.

A double raise in your partner's suit shows strong support (at least four

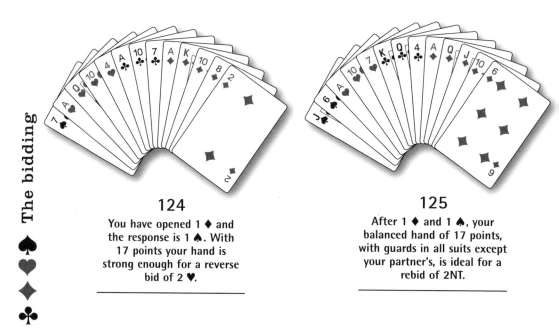

124

You have opened 1 ♦ and the response is 1 ♠. With 17 points your hand is strong enough for a reverse bid of 2 ♥.

125

After 1 ♦ and 1 ♠, your balanced hand of 17 points, with guards in all suits except your partner's, is ideal for a rebid of 2NT.

cards) in his suit. Since you have such a strong suit between you, you can shade the points requirement to 15 if your support is particularly strong. Figure 127 shows such a hand. Clearly there is a strong possibility of a game, which your partner will bid unless very weak.

(d) Rebids to Game or Game-forcing

If you hold a hand of 19 or more points, or have very good distribution, you can rebid straight to game, in your own or your partner's suit or in no-trumps, or jump in a new suit – forcing to game. Figures 128 and 129 (see page 108) show examples.

Rebid after a shift at the two level

When your partner has responded with a shift at the Two level, but it is still the lowest level, in sequences like 1 ♥ and 2 ♦ or 1 ♥ and 2 ♣, then the opener's response obeys the principles set out for responses at the One level, with one exception. You cannot bid 1NT, to show a balanced hand, but must respond 2NT, and need more high-card points – you should have 16–18 points. Your partner should have around nine for his response, so you are in the range of game. Your partner, if his hand is suitable, can raise to 3NT, or if he is one-suited repeat his suit.

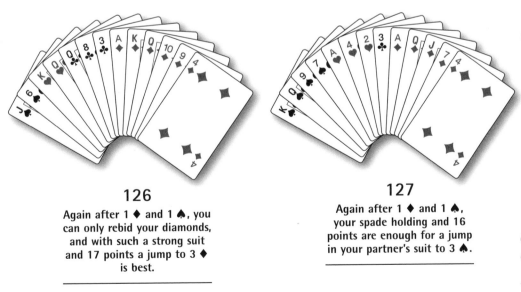

126

Again after 1 ♦ and 1 ♠, you can only rebid your diamonds, and with such a strong suit and 17 points a jump to 3 ♦ is best.

127

Again after 1 ♦ and 1 ♠, your spade holding and 16 points are enough for a jump in your partner's suit to 3 ♠.

128

You opened 1 ♦ and your partner responded 1 ♥. You are strong enough, with 19 points and a singleton, to bid game at 4 ♥.

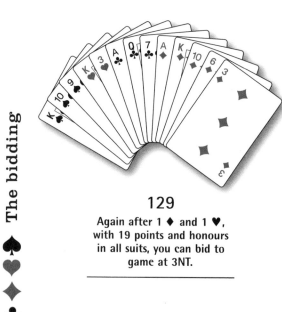

129

Again after 1 ♦ and 1 ♥, with 19 points and honours in all suits, you can bid to game at 3NT.

Rebid after a jump in a new suit

If the responder jumps in a new suit, in sequences like 1 ♥ to 3 ♦ or 1 ♦ to 2 ♠, then this is forcing to game. You know your partner has around 16 points and a game of some sort must be on. The rebidding policy here is to rebid as you would have done had the responder not jumped. For example, if you opened 1 ♦ and the response is a jump shift to 2 ♠, bid the suit you would have but at the necessarily higher level. So if you would have rebid 2 ♦ over a response of 1 ♠, rebid 3 ♦. If you opened 1 ♠, intending to bid 2 ♥ over a response of 1 ♣ or 1 ♦, bid 3 ♥ if the response is 2 ♣ or 2 ♦. Even with a stronger than minimum hand, there is no need to jump yourself since the responder's bid has already obliged both partners not to pass before game is reached. You can explore slam possibilities once the trump suit is agreed.

Bidding to slam

We have looked at opening the bidding, responding and rebids. One could go on and on: 'If I bid this, and partner responds that, and I rebid this and partner then bids that, what do I bid then?' Fortunately, the possibilities become so numerous that instinct has to take over from formula. However, there are still devices that partners can use to help them find the right contract as they approach the bonus-reaping levels of small and grand slams.

As stated in an earlier section, the combined high-card points requirement for a small slam is 33 points. This is the minimum number you can have and you must be sure that you and your partner have at least three Aces.

How do you know if you are in the slam zone? If you are sitting opposite a partner who opens 2 ♣ (23 points or more), and you are holding a hand with, say, 11 points, you know immediately that there are possibilities of a slam. Similarly, if your partner opens Two of any suit other than clubs, and you hold an opening hand of 15 points or so, you are alerted to slam chances. If you open the bidding with a strong hand of around 19 points as in Figure 130 – a hand on which you would have forced as responder – and your partner forces with a jump, say to 3 ♦, implying he has 16 points, you are in slam range.

Suppose your partner opens and to your response makes a jump rebid, while at the same time you are holding a strong opening hand. You know you are at or approaching slam level. For example, you hold the hand in Figure 131, and your partner opens 1 ♦. You respond 1 ♠ and he rebids 3 ♦, a jump raise in his own suit, suggesting a strong diamond suit and 16 points or more. As you hold 15 points, you have at least 31 points between you, and can enquire about a slam. Were your partner to be holding the hand shown in Figure 126 (see page 107), a slam may be on.

130

You have opened 1 ♠ with 19 points and your partner has responded with a jump to 3 ♦. You know he has around 16 points and a slam is a possibility.

131

You hold 15 points and respond 1 ♠ to your partner's opening 1 ♦. When he rebids 3 ♦ you can see possibilities of a slam.

♠
♥
♦
♣

Also, of course, if partner rebids 3NT over your response at the One level, he must be holding a hand of 19 points. If you hold a hand of 15 points, you can bid straight to 6NT, as you can count 34 points between you. Suppose your partner's hand is the one in Figure 129 (see page 108), and he opens 1 ♦. Your hand is that in Figure 132 and you respond 1 ♥. Your partner then rebids 3NT. You can bid straight to 6NT, and if you consider the two hands, you can see that you have an excellent chance of making a slam, if only with the fifth club or a spade finesse (which will explained shortly).

There are two aids you can use in the final stages of a bidding to a slam, cue bids and Blackwood.

Cue bids
The first thing to be decided on the way to a slam is the denomination. Once that has been decided, a bid of a new suit at the Four level is a cue bid, which shows your partner that you have first-round control of that suit. This can mean that you hold the Ace, or have a void and will be able to trump in it.

Look at the two hands in Figure 133. East opens the bidding with 1 ♣ and West responds 1 ♠. East double raises to 3 ♠, agreeing a trump suit. West's bid of 4 ♦ is cue bid, showing first-round control of diamonds, and asking if East has control of hearts. East bids 4 ♥, also a cue bid, showing he does.

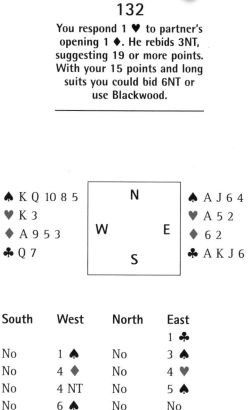

132

You respond 1 ♥ to partner's opening 1 ♦. He rebids 3NT, suggesting 19 or more points. With your 15 points and long suits you could bid 6NT or use Blackwood.

♠ K Q 10 8 5	N	♠ A J 6 4
♥ K 3		♥ A 5 2
♦ A 9 5 3	W E	♦ 6 2
♣ Q 7	S	♣ A K J 6

South	West	North	East
			1 ♣
No	1 ♠	No	3 ♠
No	4 ♦	No	4 ♥
No	4 NT	No	5 ♠
No	6 ♠	No	No
No			

133

The hands and bidding as described in the text, indicating a cue bid and Blackwood.

West can bid 4NT to ask how many Aces East has and East responds 5 ♠, indicating three. Knowing his side holds all the Aces, around 32 points and probably nine spades, West can bid 6 ♠, and the contract should be made. The bid of 4NT is called Blackwood (see below), which is the second main aid in the final stages of slam bidding.

Blackwood

The Blackwood convention, invented by an American player, Easley Blackwood, in 1933, is used when a potential slam bidder is missing a vital Ace or two and needs to know how many Aces his partner holds. He solves this by bidding 4NT. His partner gives him the information by bidding as follows:

With no Aces or four Aces, 5 ♣
With one Ace, 5 ♦
With two Aces, 5 ♥
With three Aces, 5 ♠

If the player who bid 4NT now bids 5NT, he is asking how many Kings are held, and is answered in the same manner as above, with responses of 6 ♣, 6 ♦, 6 ♥, 6 ♠.

Another typical example of the use of Blackwood is shown by the hands in Figure 134. West opened 1 ♠, and East, with 17 points, made the cheapest bid of 2 ♣, which is forcing for one round. West showed his second suit with 2 ♥, showing at least four hearts. East with 3 ♥ agreed hearts as the trump suit and West made a cheap bid of 4 ♣ showing values in East's first bid suit. East, knowing the partnership had 30 points or more and sensing a slam, asked West how many Aces he held by bidding 4NT. West's 5 ♦ answered 'one'. East would have signed off with a bid of 5 ♥ had West denied an Ace, but West's Ace led East to bid 6 ♥. Unless the hearts split badly, the slam should be made.

If you refer back to Figures 114 and 115 (see page 101), the accompanying text stated that the partnership should reach a small slam, with the help of Blackwood. After the bidding described there (1 ♠, 2NT, 3 ♣ and 4 ♣) it

	♠ A K Q 9 5	N		♠ 10
	♥ Q 10 8 2	W E		♥ A K J 5
	♦ 5			♦ K 8 7 4
	♣ K J 7	S		♣ A Q 8 3

South	West	North	East
	1 ♠	No	2 ♣
No	2 ♥	No	2 ♥
No	4 ♣	No	4 NT
No	5 ♦	No	6 ♥
No	No	No	

134
The Blackwood convention in operation.

♠
♥
♦
♣

could proceed 4NT (Blackwood),
5 ♥ (two Aces) and 6 ♣. The slam
is a certainty (indeed 7 ♣ or 7NT
is on).

Beware of over-using Blackwood.
Beginners tend to bid Blackwood as
routine when the reply won't help them.
Sometimes it is necessary to know if
your partner holds a specific Ace rather
than how many, which Blackwood
won't necessarily reveal.

If you use Blackwood you must also
be able to cope with any responses you
might get. If your agreed suit is clubs,
make sure one missing Ace is all you
need for a slam bid, because your
partner's response of 5 ♦, indicating he
holds an Ace, has already forced you
into the small slam.

Making a slam is one of the big
thrills in Bridge, but you should be
aware of your chances when bidding
it. Remember, if you are contemplating
a slam you probably have a certain
game at your mercy, so the penalty
for failing to make the slam is not just
the penalty you give the other side but
also the game you miss yourself.
This amounts to about the same as
the bonus you would get for the slam,
so slams should not be bid on anything
much less than an even chance. Do
not be disappointed therefore if you
fail to bid some slams that you might
have made. It is better to be sure
of making most of the slams that
you do bid.

Defensive bidding

We have considered bidding so far only
from the point of view of one side. But
of course the bidding might be
competitive, with both sides bidding at
once. It might be that both sides think
they have the balance of power and
both want to reach a contract. Of course
it is quite possible that both sides *could*
make a contract, bearing in mind that
the contracting side chooses trumps.
Sometimes, however, one side can
realize they are weaker, but still bid in
order to impede their opponents'
bidding. By interfering they can disrupt
the opponents' dialogue, causing them
to reach the wrong contract. They might
force the opponents to bid too high, and
contract to make more tricks than they
can or, conversely, they might scare
opponents into stopping too early and
missing a makable game. They might
even steal the contract themselves.

Also, even if the opponents seem
certain to win the auction, a side can
still conduct its own dialogue, and
can suggest opening leads against the
opponents' contract.

When one side opens the bidding, the
other side's players are the *defenders*, no
matter what the ultimate outcome of the
auction. Of course, this description
applies to the auction only – should the
defenders actually win the auction, the
other side become defenders in play.

The defenders in the auction must
be careful in their bidding. Just as in

auctions for works of art or other goods, people who bid merely to push the price up risk winning the auction and getting something they didn't really want.

There are two main ways in which the defending side can contest auctions. One is with the *double* and the other the *overcall*.

The double

The most common way for the defending side to enter the auction is by means of the *take-out double*. When the double was first introduced into Bridge, it was purely a device for the defending side to double the stakes when they thought they could beat the contract. The purpose of the double was to double the penalty incurred by the opponents for failure. It is now known as a *penalty double* to distinguish it from a take-out double. The contracting side then acquired the right to redouble if they were confident of making their contract. Doubling and redoubling were used only when the contracts got high – there was no point in doubling the early exploratory bids, which were clearly going to be superseded.

In about 1912 some players began to use the double during the first round of bidding to send a message to their partners. This was not intended to be the final call but was a request to a partner to bid – in effect to take out the double. It is therefore a convention, and is widely used.

It is used when the opponent to your right has opened the bidding in a suit and you hold a hand strong in the other three suits. You double, which asks your partner to name his strongest suit of those unbid. Consider the hand shown in Figure 135. The dealer, to your right, opens 1 ♦. Had he not opened, you would have opened. By doubling, you pass the message to your partner that you have values for an opening bid yourself and can support all of the other three suits. You are asking him to bid his strongest suit.

Your distribution need not be 4–4–4–1 or 5–4–4–0. Provided you will not be embarrassed by any suit that your partner names, you are in a good

135

Opponent to your right has opened 1 ♦. You double – a take-out double asking your partner to bid his best suit.

position to call a take-out double. For example, with the hand in Figure 136, you would have only three-card support for your partner in clubs or hearts, but by bidding spades on your next round would give him a good picture of your hand.

In some situations it is difficult to distinguish between a penalty double and a take-out double. The thing to remember is that if one partner has already bid, then a take-out double is pointless, as you already know his best suit. So doubles made when a partner has bid are for penalties. If a partner has not made a bid (passes do not count as bids) then a double is for take-out.

Responses to a take-out double

If your partner makes a take-out double, there are only two situations where you may pass. One is if your hand is worthless and your right-hand opponent has bid immediately after your partner has doubled and so has taken out the double. The other situation is if your only strong suit is the one bid, when you can make a penalty pass (i.e. the take-out double becomes one for penalties). But you need something like six cards headed by an honour or two to make this pass. Remember, your partner probably holds one trump at most.

Otherwise, the responses to a take-out double are:

(a) With a weak hand (seven or fewer points) make a minimum call

136
You can double a bid of 1 ♦ and, over a response from your partner in clubs or hearts, bid your spades.

in your longest suit, or if you have a guard in the opponent's suit, 1NT.
(b) With a better hand (about eight to ten points), make a jump in your longest suit, or if you have a guard in the opponent's suit, 2NT.
(c) With a strong hand, where – taking into account your partner's hand – making game is almost certain, make a bid in the opponent's suit.

Examples of *(b)* and *(c)* are shown in Figures 137 and 138. With the hand in Figure 137 the partnership is may hold no fewer than 23 points and eight trumps – your partner can bid 4 ♠ unless he doubled on a minimum hand with only three spades. In Figure 138, the combined points are likely to be more like 27, with a shortage in hearts. You may be missing no more than a King in the other three suits, and there is plenty of bidding space to find the best denomination for game.

137

After your partner has
doubled 1 ♥, you can
bid 2 ♠.

The overcall

An overcall is a bid of a suit, or no-trumps, over an opponent's bid. While a take-out double is competitive and might lead to your side winning the contract, overcalls are used mainly to disrupt the opposition bidding. It is of course important to be careful that you do not risk incurring a penalty double, particularly if you are vulnerable.

(a) Simple overcall A simple overcall is made at the lowest possible level over the opponent's suit. It does not need such a good hand as the normal opening bid, and can be made with as few as eight points, the typical range being 8–12, but it is made with as many as 16 points. However, you are promising your partner a reasonably good five-card suit, one with at least two honours.

A hand suitable for a simple overcall at the level of One is shown in Figure 139. The opener has bid 1 ♦. You can bid 1 ♠ to cut down your opponents'

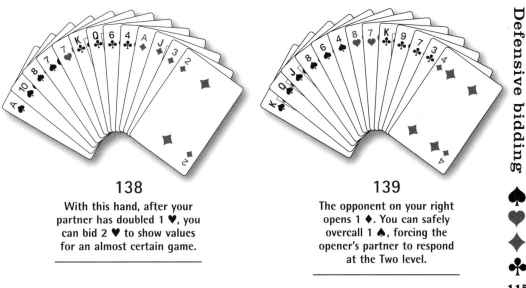

138

With this hand, after your
partner has doubled 1 ♥, you
can bid 2 ♥ to show values
for an almost certain game.

139

The opponent on your right
opens 1 ♦. You can safely
overcall 1 ♠, forcing the
opener's partner to respond
at the Two level.

bidding space. Your strong spades mean that going down in a doubled contract will not be too disastrous and if your partner is strong you may even win the contract in spades. Also, in the unlikely event of your opponents reaching a contract in 3NT, your partner has been signalled a spade lead.

A hand not suitable for an overcall is one that has good defensive values – stoppers in many suits but with no strong suit of its own.

If you have to overcall at the level of Two, you need about 12 points and a five-card suit, or 11 points and a six-card suit. Obviously at that level you need to make eight tricks and going three or four down doubled is expensive. The hand in Figure 140 is one where an overcall at that level is justified. With 15 points and seven tricks likely in trumps and spades you cannot come to too much harm in overcalling 2 ♣.

It is reasonable to make a simple overcall in the fourth position in the bidding round, but if your partner has passed, you must take his weakness into consideration.

(b) Jump overcalls A jump overcall, overcalling at one level higher than is necessary, requires a stronger hand, say 12–16 points, and a five or six-card suit. The same precautions apply as for a simple overcall, and the shape of the hand is as vital. Figure 141 shows a hand where a jump overcall is in order.

140

Again your right-hand opponent opens 1 ♦. With 15 points you are justified in overcalling 2 ♣.

141

After an opening 1 ♦ on your right, you could overcall 2 ♠ on this 15-pointer, forcing your opponents to bid at the Three level.

The bidding

♠
♥
♦
♣

116

(c) Overcalls of 1NT If you have a strong balanced hand of 16–18 points – the sort of hand with which you could open 1NT – then 1NT is the best overcall you can make. Figure 142 shows a typical hand for a 1NT overcall. Your opponent has bid 1 ♥ and you have two honours in hearts as a guard in that suit. Suppose, however, the ♠ 8 and 7 were the ♥ 8 and 7, giving you five cards in your opponent's suit. It might be a better tactic to make a pass, called a *trap pass*. The opponents cannot have more than 22 points, as you hold 18, and your side might easily have the balance of power. To allow the opponents to get into a contract they cannot make, especially if they are vulnerable, and you get the chance to double it, might bring good rewards.

142

Your right-hand opponent has opened 1 ♥. With 18 points and a balanced hand, including a guard in hearts, you can overcall with 1NT.

Responses to overcalls

When responding to your partner's overcall in a suit, with an intervening pass from your second opponent, it is usually best to support your partner's suit or bid no-trumps. A response of 1NT requires 8–11 points, a balanced hand, and a guard in opponent's suit. With a weak hand (3–7 points) but three-card support for your partner's suit (giving your side eight cards in that suit), it is usually best to raise his suit by one (1 ♠ to 2 ♠). If you have four-card support, giving you nine trumps between you, raise partner's suit by two. You may go down, but you have

probably stopped your opponents making a game. With no better than a doubleton in your partner's suit, it is probably best to pass.

It is easy to judge your response to a partner who overcalls 1NT. He has 16–18 points, the same as if he opened 1NT naturally, so you can respond in the same manner.

Sacrifice bids

Occasionally, where your opponents look to have values that would ensure them the game, particularly if the game would give them the rubber, it is useful for a side to sacrifice, which means they bid to make a contract they know they cannot achieve. The justification is

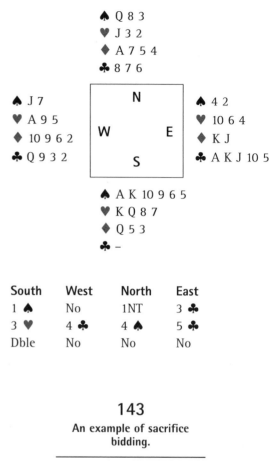

	♠ Q 8 3	
	♥ J 3 2	
	♦ A 7 5 4	
	♣ 8 7 6	

♠ J 7	N	♠ 4 2
♥ A 9 5		♥ 10 6 4
♦ 10 9 6 2	W E	♦ K J
♣ Q 9 3 2	S	♣ A K J 10 5

	♠ A K 10 9 6 5	
	♥ K Q 8 7	
	♦ Q 5 3	
	♣ –	

South	West	North	East
1 ♠	No	1NT	3 ♣
3 ♥	4 ♣	4 ♠	5 ♣
Dble	No	No	No

143
An example of sacrifice bidding.

that you incur fewer penalty points than the opponents would make if they took the rubber.

A hand in which a sacrifice is a good tactic is shown in Figure 143. North/South are vulnerable. After South and North had opened calmly, North's 1NT being based on a balanced seven points, East decided the strength was with North/South and pre-empted with 3 ♣. South enquired about North's hearts, and West, although having only seven points, upped the pre-empt to 4 ♣. North bravely showed his partner his preference for spades over hearts with 4 ♠ and East, not expecting to make the contract, but guessing North/South had the cards for game in spades, made the final sacrifice bid of 5 ♣. South saw too many gaps in his hearts and diamonds suits to risk going further and doubled instead. East/West will probably go three down in 5 ♣ for a penalty of 500, a reasonable result when North/South could have taken the rubber in a contract of 4 ♠.

Bidding: summary
If you have read all this section on bidding you will have realized what a complicated thing it can be. It provokes more discussion at the table than anything and the prospect of studying it is what puts off most would-be players. But it is all very logical, and easily picked up when you start to play. Do not worry if you and your partner occasionally get your wires crossed and end up in silly contracts or miss a slam from time to time, because these things happen to experts as well.

There is no need to think, as you begin to play, that you must know all the points requirements needed for every bid you make or all the nuances of every response partner makes. It is impossible to play Bridge by formula. Bridge was played and enjoyed long before all these 'rules', which are really only recommendations, were invented. So, you open the bidding with a hand of 13 points, or perhaps 12 if the distribution is good? That is sensible advice, but what did Bridge players do before Milton Work devised the high-card point count? They used their instinct, and the best Bridge players are those who can use their instinct as well as play by the book.

Even so, you will have realized how important the high-card point count actually is. It would be quite impossible to discuss the techniques of playing the game of Bridge without it. It is one of the aids to good bidding invented over the years, together with the many other bidding conventions.

On the other hand, you will have grasped that if you and your partner are going to play Bridge well, you must have some sort of system that you both understand and obey. There is no point whatsoever in misleading your partner. You must trust each other. If you start thinking 'My partner's made a mistake here, I must do something to rescue the situation', your bidding goes haywire and you are heading for disaster.

Bidding conventions

As a checklist, here is a review of the few artificial bids that we recommend in this book.

(a) The 2 ♣ opening bid This is used to open the bidding with a very strong hand, usually of 23 or more points, but the point count could be reduced a little if the distribution is good.

(b) The pre-emptive bid This is a bid of Three or Four in a suit made with a weak hand of, say, 6–10 points, but with, perhaps, a seven-card suit. It is a bid to obstruct the opponents, who might have the stronger hands, forcing them to begin bidding at a high level.

(c) The take-out double This bid is made over an opening suit bid by an opponent which tells your partner that you have a hand good enough to open with yourself (13 points or more) with good cards in the unbid suits and usually a shortage in the bid suit.

(d) The Stayman convention This is used when your partner has opened 1NT. It is made when you have a good hand including at least four cards in a major suit in which game is likely, provided partner holds four cards in the suit. A bid of 2 ♣ is a request for partner to bid a four-card major suit. If he has none, he bids 2 ♦.

(e) The Blackwood convention This is used when, in order to discover the prospects for a slam, you need to know how many Aces your partner holds. This is done with a bid of 4NT. Your partner responds 5 ♣ with none or four Aces, 5 ♦ with one, 5 ♥ with two and 5 ♠ with three. If necessary, he can be asked how many Kings he holds with a bid of 5NT, the replies being 6 ♣ to 6 ♠, on the same principle.

THE PLAY 3

THE
PLAY

• •

Most people who decide to learn to play Bridge have played other card games, including trick-taking games. They will clearly have knowledge of how to make the most of their hands, and might think this section is of little interest. They would be very wrong. Bridge is unlike other commonly played card games in that it features an exposed dummy. All three players taking part in the play, therefore, know the contents of two of the four hands, their own and the dummy's. They know, in fact, where half the cards in the pack are. From the bidding they might have drawn inferences about the composition of the other two hands as well. We will consider what this means first from the point of view of the declarer.

The declarer's play

The declarer knows all 26 cards that his side holds, and in fact it is his duty to play them. By inference, of course, he knows all 26 cards that the opponent's hold. All he doesn't know is which of the two defenders holds which of those cards. But there are methods he can use

to cut out unnecessary guesswork and improve his chances of success.

Deciding a strategy

When the dummy is placed on the table, it is in order to take a minute or two to study the dummy and plan a course of action. The declarer knows how many tricks he has to make and should work out the possibilities of how to make them. Similarly the defenders should note any weaknesses there might be in the dummy, but the declarer has the best chance to form plans. For example, consider the two hands, the declarer's and the dummy's in Figure 144. West is the declarer in 3NT, North leads ♦ 2 and East's hand is laid on the table as the dummy. West estimates his tricks. He has five tricks 'on top' (i.e. five unbeatable winners): ♠ A, K, ♥ A, ♦ A and K. The helpful lead of the ♦ 2 ensured a sixth trick, because West will win the trick with either the ♦ A or ♦ J, depending on whether or not South plays ♦ Q. In either case the ♦ J will be a sixth winner.

Where will the other three tricks come from? He can clearly make two tricks from clubs, and he will need to make his ninth trick from ♠ J by means of a finesse (see page 123) or from a 'long' spade or club – that is, by having the only spade or club left when three rounds have been played. The danger is that his opponents might attack his weak suit, hearts, where he can win only one trick, with the Ace. His opponents could take

♠ A K J 3   ♠ 9 6 4
♥ 7 6 4   ♥ A 5 3
♦ A J 4   ♦ K 8 5
♣ K 3 2   ♣ Q J 5 4

144

West is the declarer in 3NT. North leads ♦ 2. The declarer's strategy is discussed in the text.

---

three or four heart tricks before he can establish his club tricks or his third spade trick.

The declarer's strategy must be to win the opening diamond lead in his hand (West), and then to lead a low club to the ♣ Q. If the defence takes the Ace, the declarer has established his two club tricks. If the defence does not play the Ace this round, the declarer should lead a low club again, towards the King. The idea is to take or establish two club tricks before the defence can knock out his ♥ A. Notice that if when West leads a low club to the Queen, North plays the ♣ A, then the declarer plays low from dummy and has established *three* club tricks, and his contract is safe. Similarly, if a low club is led from the dummy towards the

King, and South plays the Ace, West plays low and a third club trick is established. If the ♣ A is held up for two rounds, and neither opponent has discarded, declarer plays his last club towards ♣ J and 5. If North plays the Ace, the ♣ J is established for a third club trick. If North doesn't play the Ace, but still follows with a club, the declarer plays ♣ J from the dummy. If it loses to South's ♣ A, then declarer has established a third club trick with ♣ 5. So the worst that can happen to the declarer is that only two tricks will come from clubs, and the last trick will need to be obtained from spades.

Since the declarer knows all 26 cards that his side holds (and that he has to play), and by inference all 26 that the defenders hold, opportunities arise for skilful play, where he can seem to manufacture tricks where none appear to be. In many combinations of holdings in a particular suit, there are methods he can use to maximize his tricks in the suit, or to improve his chances of making a certain number of tricks. We have just seen how a declarer can give himself the best chance of making three tricks from the club suit holdings in Figure 144, and we will look at more examples, beginning with the best known, the simple finesse.

The finesse

Suppose, as declarer, you hold A, Q and 6 in your hand, and K, 5 and 3 in the dummy. Discounting trumps, you are certain to win three tricks in the suit, unless you are silly enough to play A and K or K and Q in the same trick. However, if you held A, Q and 6 in your hand and 5, 3 and 2 in the dummy, you are only certain to win one trick, the Ace. If you lead Ace or Queen from your hand, that is all you will make, unless you lead Ace and an opponent is holding the bare King. You can give yourself an even-money chance of winning two tricks by leading the 2 from dummy towards your A, Q. If the opponent to your right holds the King, you will make two tricks, because if he plays it, you win with Ace and the Queen becomes master. If he doesn't play the King you win with Queen and still have the Ace. Of course, if the opponent to your right doesn't have the King, you will lose the Queen to the King on your left – but you have given yourself an even chance of a second trick. This manoeuvre is called a *finesse*. You are said to be finessing against the King.

You can finesse without holding the Ace. Suppose you hold K, 8 in hand opposite 7,5. No certain tricks here, but you can give yourself an even chance of one by leading the 5 towards the K, 8. If the player on your left has the Ace, you'll make the King, because if he plays it, you play the 8 and make the King later. If he doesn't play the Ace, you play the King and win.

Look at the situation in Figure 145. You need to make three tricks, and the only way you can is to win with the Ace, King and Jack. Your best chance (slightly better than even) is to play King first. This might drop a bare Queen, and make the Ace and Jack winners. Should the Queen not fall, a small card is played towards the Ace and Jack. If East has the Queen, he either plays it and loses to the Ace, or he doesn't and the Jack wins.

Assuming split honours

One stage on from the simple finesse is the double finesse. Figure 146 shows the situation. One trick is certain with the Ace. What are the best chances of making a second? The answer is to assume *split honours* – that the King

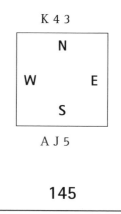

K 4 3

N

W　　　　E

S

A J 5

145

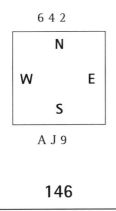

6 4 2

A J 9

146

and Queen are in separate hands. So you take the finesse against the 10 first, by leading the 2 and playing the 9. If West is forced to play, say, Queen to beat it, leaving East with King and 10, then later on, when you play 4 towards the Ace and then Jack, you will win them both. If East plays his honour, you win with Ace and later Jack – if he doesn't, then you win with first Jack then Ace. Notice that if East plays the 10 on the first round, you beat it with the Jack, which West beats with his honour. You will have the same situation when you lead the 4 – unless East plays his honour, the 9 wins.

Any combination of two cards, such as Ace and Queen, which are held over two opposing cards on your right, such as King and Jack, is known as a *tenace*.

If the suit is led through your right-hand opponent you make two tricks from the combination by beating whichever card he plays and leaving your remaining card the master (the highest card left in the suit).

Playing towards honours

Consider the situation in Figure 147. You want to make three tricks. You are certain to lose one trick to the Ace, and are certain to make two from K, Q and J. If the defending players each hold three of the missing cards in the suit (Bridge players describe this by saying, 'If the suit breaks 3–3') then your third trick will come from the fourth club in South's hand. It is more likely (64 per cent to 36 per cent) that the suit will not break 3–3. You can still make three

4 3 2

K Q J 5

147

♠
♥
♦
♣

tricks from the suit, if East has the Ace, which will happen in half of that 64 per cent. You lead from the North hand towards the honours in the South hand, two or three times if needed. If East plays Ace on any of these leads you play 5 from South. The Ace is wasted on two small cards and K, Q and J win tricks. By leading towards the honours in Figure 147, you will make three tricks 68 per cent of the time.

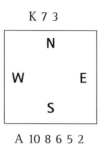

K 7 3

A 10 8 6 5 2

148

The value of low cards
When you have a long suit, you can win tricks with low cards. Consider the holdings in Figure 148. The only honours in the two hands are Ace and King, but the partnership holds nine cards in the suit. This means that the defence holds only four. If these four cards split 2–2, which they will do 46 per cent of the time, by winning two tricks with Ace and King you will have cleared your opponents' hands of the suit, and can make four more tricks with the low cards remaining in South's hand. Only in fewer than 10 per cent of occasions will one of the opposing hands hold all four missing cards, in which case you might lose two tricks to Queen and Jack, but that still leaves two tricks to be won with your low cards.

Sometimes with a long suit missing some honours you will have to concede tricks in the suit in order to *promote* low cards as winners. With the North/South cards in Figure 149 you

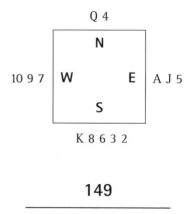

Q 4

10 9 7   A J 5

K 8 6 3 2

149

The play
♠
♥
♦
♣

hold seven of the suit, but without the Ace, Jack and 10. If the six missing cards are split 3–3, as shown, you can still win three tricks from the suit. Lead towards the Queen in the North hand. East will take the Ace, but next time you have the lead, win with the King and lead another to lose to the Jack. You are left with the only two cards in the suit, the 3 and 2 – both winners. It doesn't matter when East takes his Ace – you must make either the King or Queen plus the two long cards.

Drawing trumps

When playing in a trump contract, you and your partner will hold more trumps than the defence (or you wouldn't have chosen that suit as trumps). One of the first decisions a declarer has to make is whether or not to *draw trumps* – to lead trumps until the defence has none left. The point of drawing trumps is to ensure that the defence is unable to trump any of your winners, while you retain a trump or two yourself. It is often right to draw trumps, and generally speaking you should do so unless there is a good reason not to. You should avoid drawing trumps when doing so might exhaust the dummy as well as your opponents of trumps, and you hold a loser or two in your hand which you need to trump in the dummy. You might also need a trump in dummy as an entry (see page 129) to dummy in order to cash a winner there.

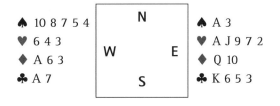

150

East is the declarer in 4 ♥ and South leads ♦ 2. East must attempt to trump a club in the dummy before drawing trumps.

An example of the first instance is shown in Figure 150. East is the declarer in 4 ♥. A low diamond is led from South, and dummy is revealed. East can see immediately he is likely to lose one or possibly two trump tricks and a spade. The diamond lead is excellent, as it gives two winners in the suit (he ducks (see page 131) in the dummy and, whether or not North plays the King, the Queen and Ace are winners). There are two losers in clubs, however, and the declarer's first priority must be to try to trump them with dummy's small trumps. Suppose the ♦ Q wins the opening trick. A small club is led to the dummy's Ace, and the

♠
♥
♦
♣

♣ 7 returned to ♣ K. A third club is then led and trumped in the dummy (the declarer must assume clubs break 4–3). A return to hand with the ♥ A and a fourth club is lead. This cannot win, but at worst must draw a trump from the defence, reducing its trumps to four, and giving the declarer a better chance to pick up the King or Queen of trumps when he leads them. His contract is not safe, but he has given himself the best chance to succeed.

The crossruff

The need to keep trumps in dummy for trumping losers from hand is at its most obvious when the contract can best be won by *crossruffing*.

The two hands shown in Figure 151 form a good example. As South you are the declarer in 4 ♥, and the defence begins by leading ♦ A, K and J – the last of which you trump with ♥ 6. You have lost two tricks and look certain to lose a club, so you can afford to lose no more. Should you draw trumps you could end up with only eight tricks, but by using your trumps to trump losers in each hand alternately you cannot fail to make your contract as long as the ♠ A, K and ♣ A are not trumped.

The strategy to use is the crossruff, by which you use your trumps in each hand to trump, or ruff, the losers in the other. First make the ♠ A and K, then lead a low club to ♣ A. You now have

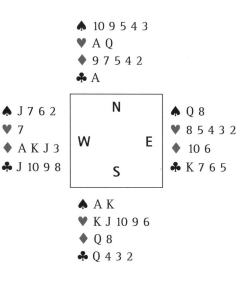

151

South is in 4 ♥ and loses the first two tricks to ♦ A, K. Despite East's five trumps, South makes his contract with a crossruff.

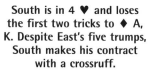

four tricks, and you hold the six highest trumps, and can make them all. You lead ♦ 7, trumped in your hand, ♣ 3, trumped in the dummy with ♥ Q, the ♦ 9, trumped in your hand, the ♣ 4, trumped with ♥ A in the dummy, and the ♠ 5, trumped with ♥ J in your hand. You now have nine tricks and the ♥ K makes the tenth. You have your contract despite East holding five trumps against you. If you lay out the cards and play out the hand, you will find East's trumps fall beneath your winning trumps, although he wins the last trick.

Establishing a suit in dummy

Sometimes you might need to hold up the drawing of trumps in order to use a trump or two in the dummy as entries. For example, look at the hands in Figure 152. West is the declarer in 4 ♠, and the defence reels off the first three tricks in hearts. Clubs are then led and the declarer makes his Ace. He cannot afford to lose another trick, but the only way he can avoid losing a club is to establish the dummy's diamonds in order to discard the last club in his

hand. He cannot draw trumps as the only entries he has in the dummy to lead diamonds are ♦ A and trumps. His policy must be to cash ♦ K, and lead to ♦ A. He must then lead ♦ 9. If South trumps he must overtrump. If South follows suit he must trump high with ♠ A. If diamonds break 3–3, the declarer will have established ♦ 10 on which he can park his losing ♣ 4. Once the ♦ 10 is established, he can then draw three rounds of trumps ending with ♠ Q, which provides an entry to the established ♦ 10. On the other hand, if there is still a diamond outstanding, the declarer must enter the dummy again by leading to ♠ Q. He then leads another diamond from the dummy and trumps it with whatever trump is necessary to be certain of winning the trick (it could be ♠ K). The dummy's diamond is now finally established, and the declarer can draw a second round of trumps before leading to ♠ 10 to cash his long diamond. Only if trumps break 4–0 in the North hand will the declarer be foiled of his contract.

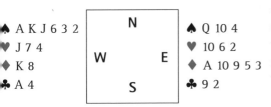

♠ A K J 6 3 2   ♠ Q 10 4
♥ J 7 4   ♥ 10 6 2
♦ K 8   ♦ A 10 9 5 3
♣ A 4   ♣ 9 2

152
West is declarer in 4 ♠ but loses three heart tricks immediately. He must establish a third diamond trick on which to park his ♣ 4 before drawing trumps.

Entries and unblocking

The means of getting from one hand to the other is one which often crops up in Bridge, and sometimes tricks are lost through carelessness. Usually it is a question of tricks being established in the dummy, but with no way of getting to the dummy to cash them. What the dummy lacks is an entry. In Figure 153

♠
♥
♦
♣

the declarer, South, is hoping to make 3NT and needs to make all five club tricks. The suit is divided as shown, and provided the suit does not break 4–0 he is sure to make them. But suppose he has used all his entries to dummy apart from the clubs and begins by playing ♣ 3 to ♣ A, returns ♣ 2 to ♣ K and because the suit was 3–1 and ♣ J hasn't fallen, he plays ♣ 6 to ♣ Q. Suddenly one of his tricks has vanished. He must lead ♣ 7 or ♣ 4 to ♣ 9 in his hand, but the fifth club remains isolated in the dummy. The mistake could easily have been avoided at trick three by playing the ♣ 9 to the ♣ Q. Then ♣ 7 would have won trick four and ♣ 4 would have won trick five.

Sometimes it is necessary to play a high card from your hand as a loser in order to protect an entry to dummy. Suppose, as South, you have the holding shown in Figure 154, and need to make four tricks in the suit, but there are no other entries to dummy. You can do this if the suit breaks 3–2 among the defenders, and the Ace is one of the two. First lead the 3 towards the Queen. The defence, realizing you are trying to establish tricks in the dummy, holds up the Ace and lets the Queen win. Return the 5 towards the King, and play the King, whatever East plays, even the Ace. Suppose you play 6 instead of King. It remains in your hand as a winner, but you have lost the chance of reaching the dummy for any others. The suit is *blocked*. By playing the King, you are unblocking, allowing you to get to the Jack and 8 in the dummy as winners.

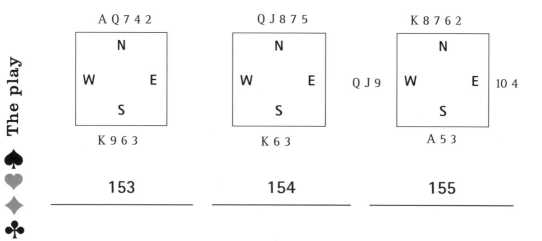

Ducking play

Another technique to reach long tricks in dummy is the ducking play. To *duck* is to decline to win a trick that you could win. It is used to set up more tricks in the suit. In Figure 155, South is in 3NT and requires at least three tricks from the suit shown, with entries to dummy limited. He has Ace and King, but if he plays them immediately, he is certain to leave the master card in the suit in the hands of the defenders – in this case the Queen in the hand of West. South will make only two tricks from the suit. South relies on the suit breaking 3–2, which it will in two out of three cases. He begins by playing Ace, and then plays a small card towards the dummy. However, instead of playing the King, he ducks, allowing West's Jack to win. When South next has the lead, he plays his last small card to the dummy's King, picking up West's Queen on the way, and has two more tricks in the suit to follow, making four in the suit.

Hold–up play

We have seen how tricks can be won with small cards in a long suit, and how it is often necessary to manage the long suit, by knocking out high cards, or stoppers, that the defence might hold, or by carefully preserving entries in order to reach the winners in the long suit.

In a no-trump contract, it is often the case that declarer and defenders all have long suits, and each will try to establish his long suit before the other. The defence in a no-trump contract will usually lead its long suit first, and it becomes necessary for the declarer, who will have a stopper in the suit, to time his use of it carefully. A *stopper* is a card in the opponents' suit that can stop the opponents running off a series of winners in it. For example, a holding of Ace, or King and Queen in an opponents' suit provides a stopper, and King and 2 holding provides a stopper so far as the declarer is concerned if the suit is led up to him on the first trick.

Often, in a no-trump contract, timing when to play the stopper is vital. Consider the four hands in Figure 156 (see page 132). South is the declarer in 3NT. West leads the ♥ 8 (against a no-trump contract it is often best for the opening lead to be fourth-highest of the longest suit, as will be explained later). South can count only five top tricks (four Aces and ♦ K). A sixth could be made from ♠ Q and J, but where will the other three come from?

South realizes that if clubs break 3–2 with split honours, he can make four extra tricks from clubs. The danger, however, is West's hearts. West could well have started with five or six hearts. As the declarer, South can see that he

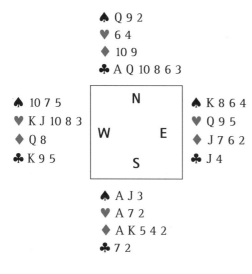

♠ Q 9 2
♥ 6 4
♦ 10 9
♣ A Q 10 8 6 3

♠ 10 7 5
♥ K J 10 8 3
♦ Q 8
♣ K 9 5

N
W E
S

♠ K 8 6 4
♥ Q 9 5
♦ J 7 6 2
♣ J 4

♠ A J 3
♥ A 7 2
♦ A K 5 4 2
♣ 7 2

156

**South is the declarer in 3NT
and ♥ 8 is lead. South must
hold up ♥ A until the
third round.**

can make only one heart, with the Ace.
Four or five hearts to the defence, plus a
club, would defeat the contract. So the
declarer must take the greatest care to
prevent West getting in again after he
takes his ♥ A. The way to do this is to
hold up the Ace.

The declarer therefore allows East's
♥ Q to win the first trick, and when
East returns a heart he allows West to
win (♥ 10 would be sufficient). West

then leads ♥ K, which South takes with
his Ace. He now leads the ♣ 2 towards
the dummy, and takes a double finesse
by playing ♣ 10, which loses to East's
♣ J. It would have been possible for
both East and West still to hold a heart,
but that does not bother declarer,
because that means that East/West can
make only one more heart trick. In the
example hand, East does not hold a
heart, so must lead another suit, the
Aces of all of which South holds.
Whatever East leads South will win in
hand and lead ♣ 7, playing for West to
hold the remaining honour, and either
playing ♣ A to beat West's ♣ K, or if
West holds back ♣ K, winning with
♣ Q. Declarer now makes five tricks from
dummy's clubs, returns to hand with
♠ A and makes ♦ K for his ninth trick
and the contract. If declarer had played
his ♥ A on either the first or second
round of the suit, he could not have
prevented the defence from taking four
heart tricks and defeating the contract.

Establishing by trumping

Sometimes a loser can be discarded by
establishing a winner in a long suit
through trumping. Figure 157 shows an
example. South, who opened 2 ♣, is
declarer in 6 ♦ and West leads ♥ 3.
South sees a potential spade loser and
club loser. But if spades break no worse
than 4–2, South can establish a fifth
spade on which to park his losing club
even though the highest spade in the

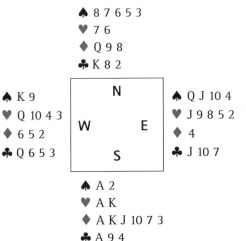

♠ 8 7 6 5 3
♥ 7 6
♦ Q 9 8
♣ K 8 2

♠ K 9
♥ Q 10 4 3
♦ 6 5 2
♣ Q 6 5 3

♠ Q J 10 4
♥ J 9 8 5 2
♦ 4
♣ J 10 7

♠ A 2
♥ A K
♦ A K J 10 7 3
♣ A 9 4

157

South is the declarer in 6 ♦ but with potential losers in spades and clubs. He can make the contract by developing the dummy's spades through trumping.

dummy's hand is ♠ 8. He does this by trumping out the spade suit. South wins the heart lead with Ace, cashes ♠ A and leads another, which he loses to West's King. It doesn't matter which suit West now leads, as the declarer holds the masters in all, but suppose West switches to a club. The declarer wins in dummy with ♣ K and leads another spade, trumped with ♦ 10 (this is to preserve entries to dummy, but as it

happens he guesses West is out of spades and if he'd trumped with ♦ 3 West would have overtrumped). The declarer now leads ♦ 3 to ♦ 8, picking up a trump from both defenders and leads another spade, trumped with ♦ J. The declarer has removed spades from the defenders' hands and established the ♠ 8 in the dummy. However, West still has two trumps, so the declarer must lead ♦ A to remove one before leading his ♦ 7 to the dummy's ♦ Q to remove the other. He then cashes ♠ 8 on which he parks ♣ 9, and returns to hand with ♥ K to make his final two tricks, and the small slam, with ♣ A and ♦ K.

Taking a chance

Sometimes you find yourself in a contract, which, after studying dummy, you realize can be made only if everything falls right for you. There's no point beating about the bush or wondering about how to reduce your penalty if things go wrong – you must go for it. Such a pair of hands is shown in Figure 158 (see page 134), with West declarer in 4 ♥. The trump suit, unless it splits badly 5–0, will bring five tricks, spades one and clubs two. Two more are required, and there is no long suit that could provide one of them. The ♠ Q and ♦ K look like the only possible saviours. So when ♠ 3 is led, West must play ♠ Q from the dummy straight away, and hope North has led from the King. This will leave one more

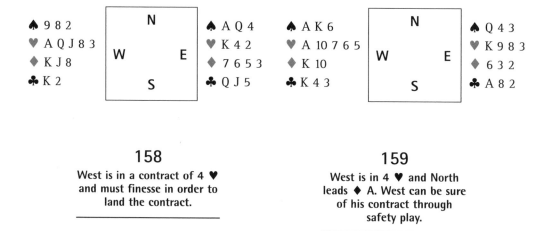

♠ 9 8 2
♥ A Q J 8 3
♦ K J 8
♣ K 2

N
W E
S

♠ A Q 4
♥ K 4 2
♦ 7 6 5 3
♣ Q J 5

♠ A K 6
♥ A 10 7 6 5
♦ K 10
♣ K 4 3

N
W E
S

♠ Q 4 3
♥ K 9 8 3
♦ 6 3 2
♣ A 8 2

158

West is in a contract of 4 ♥ and must finesse in order to land the contract.

159

West is in 4 ♥ and North leads ♦ A. West can be sure of his contract through safety play.

trick needed, which declarer can attempt by leading a diamond from dummy and playing the defenders for split honours by taking a double finesse. If Queen or Ace appear from South he will make his trick, but otherwise he plays Jack. If honours are split, it will lose to Ace or Queen, but the King is still there for another try. If North holds both Ace and Queen nothing can be done.

Safety play

Trying to conjure up an extra trick is pointless in rubber Bridge if you can make your contract by playing safe, even at the expense of losing a trick you might have won. The hands in Figure 159 provide an example. West is declarer in 4 ♥ and North leads ♦ A. It

is clear that the defence are going to win one diamond immediately and one club later. The declarer will capture the lead on the second round. He can see that once trumps are drawn, there is no danger of losing a spade, so the only way the contract could fail is if he lost two trump tricks. And the only way that could happen is if the declarer, in drawing trumps, played Ace or King on the first round and found one defender holding all four missing trumps. So he leads low to the first round of trumps – let's assume he leads ♥ 5 from his hand. As the missing trumps are Q, J, 4 and 2, the defence can win this trick only with the Queen or Jack. If the Queen or Jack appears from North, the declarer wins with King from the dummy and the defence is reduced to one trump trick at best. If North plays a low trump or discards, the declarer also plays low from the dummy. South is allowed to win with Queen or Jack if he has either. Let us say he wins with Jack, leaving the Queen outstanding. If both defenders followed suit, the Queen can now be picked up by the declarer playing Ace, then King of trumps. If North did not follow suit, then South remains holding Q, 4 and 2 and the Queen can be picked up by two finesses from the dummy. It takes a lot of words to explain, but if you lay out the declarer's and dummy's trumps as shown in Figure 159, you can dispose of the other four trumps in any way you wish between the defenders and find this strategy will always reduce losers to one. So by giving up the first trump trick, and the possibility of winning all five, the declarer makes certain of four and makes his contract.

Dummy reversal

Dummy reversal is a technique not easy for a beginner to see but it can transform the look of a hand and make contracts that looked unlikely very promising. Usually if a declarer needs to ruff a loser or two before drawing trumps, he does it in dummy, which usually has the shorter trumps. This is not always possible. However, by regarding the dummy as the master

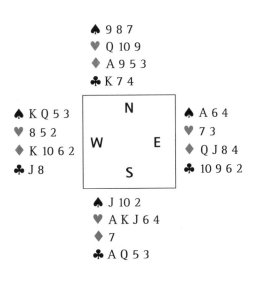

♠ 9 8 7
♥ Q 10 9
♦ A 9 5 3
♣ K 7 4

♠ K Q 5 3   N   ♠ A 6 4
♥ 8 5 2   ♥ 7 3
♦ K 10 6 2   W   E   ♦ Q J 8 4
♣ J 8   S   ♣ 10 9 6 2

♠ J 10 2
♥ A K J 6 4
♦ 7
♣ A Q 5 3

160

South is declarer in 4 ♥ but looks to have three spade losers and a club loser. By dummy reversal he can land the contract by trumping North's losing diamonds.

hand, and ruffing the dummy's losers in hand, the contract looks simpler. Consider the four hands in Figure 160. South is the declarer in 4 ♥, and can see three spade losers. If clubs break 3–3 he will make the contract, with five trumps, a diamond and four clubs. But if clubs do not break 3–3 (and the odds are against this), declarer must keep back a trump in the dummy to trump the last club. But the defence will also have a trump left, and might get in first with theirs.

If the declarer looks at the dummy as the master hand, the picture looks different. Instead of a losing clubs, the dummy has three losing diamonds. But, after the first diamond, South will be void and can trump them. Moreover he can trump them high to prevent being overtrumped. And by returning to the North hand with a trump each time, he will draw the defence's trumps, provided they break 3–2. That is a better bet (68 per cent success rate) than that clubs will break 3–3 (48 per cent success).

Assuming that the defence takes its three spade tricks immediately, and switches to a diamond, the play will go:

Trick 1
(West leads)   ♠ K, ♠ 7, ♠ 4, ♠ 2

Trick 2
(West leads)   ♠ Q, ♠ 8, ♠ 6, ♠ 10

Trick 3
(West leads)   ♠ 3, ♠ 9, ♠ A, ♠ J

Trick 4
(East leads)   ♦ 4, ♦ 7, ♦ 10, ♦ A

Trick 5
(North leads)   ♦ 3, ♦ J, ♥ A, ♦ 2

Trick 6
(South leads)   ♥ 4, ♥ 2, ♥ 9, ♥ 3

Trick 7
(North leads)   ♦ 5, ♦ 8, ♥ K, ♦ 6

Trick 8
(South leads)   ♥ 6, ♥ 5, ♥ 10, ♥ 7

Trick 9
(North leads)   ♦ 9, ♦ Q, ♥ J, ♦ K

Trick 10
(South leads)   ♣ 3, ♣ 8, ♣ K, ♣ 2

Trick 11
(North leads)   ♥ Q, ♣ 6, ♣ 5, ♥ 8

Trick 12
(North leads)   ♣ 4, ♣ 9, ♣ A, ♣ J

Trick 13
(South leads)   ♣ Q, ♠ 5, ♣ 7, ♣ 10

The contract is made by the declarer regarding his own hand as the dummy and working out how the dummy can make the contract. Had he played his hand by trying to avoid a club loser, the contract would have failed.

The defenders' play
Unlike the declarer, neither of the two defenders knows whether cards that do not appear in his own hand or the dummy are held by his side or the declarer. The defenders must try to pass information to each other during the actual play. But the defender who has to make the opening lead must do some

very careful thinking before even the
first card is laid.

The opening lead

The opening lead will depend on
whether the contract to be defeated
is in no-trumps or a suit.

(a) The opening lead at no-trumps We
know that one of the main methods of
landing a contract in no-trumps is for
the declarer to establish a long suit. The
object of the defenders must therefore
be to try to establish a long suit of their
own first. It follows that it is usual for
the opening lead against a no-trump
contract to be from the leader's longest
and strongest suit, particularly if the
defenders have not bid a suit.

The ideal holding when leading
against a no-trump contract is
something like a five- or six-card suit
headed by two or three top honours
(you are hardly likely to have anything
better because, if you had, your
opponents would not be in a no-trump
contract). Experts have worked out the
best leads from such holdings. When
you hold two or three cards in sequence
that include an honour, lead the higher
or highest of the touching cards.
Therefore with A, K and 10 lead the
Ace; from A, Q and J lead the Queen;
from Q, 10 and 9 the 10, and so on.

The main reason for this is to
prevent giving the declarer an easy trick
with a lower card. Figure 161 shows an

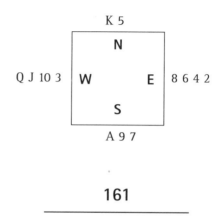

161

example. On lead as West against
South's no-trump contract, the lead of
the Queen will force the declarer to use
King or Ace to win the trick, whereas
the lead of the 3 would allow him to
win with the 9 and eventually make
three tricks in the suit.

Another reason for leading high from
the holding shown − Q, J, 10 and 3 −
is to preserve a low card to lead to your
partner if he has length. For example, in
Figure 162 (see page 138) East has the 7
held in Figure 161 by South. Now two
rounds of the suit will drive out the
declarer's Ace and King and leave the
defence with three tricks in the suit, but
only if after making the 10 West still
has the 3 to give East the lead and the
last two tricks in the suit.

It is not always the best policy to
lead one's longest suit against a no-
trump contract. If your partner has bid

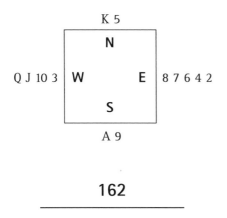

K 5

Q J 10 3   W | N / E   8 7 6 4 2

S

A 9

162

suggests to your partner a suit that might be worth attacking, but by applying what is called 'The Rule of Eleven' he can work out where the high cards in the suit lie. By subtracting the value of the card led from 11, your partner knows how many cards higher than that are shared between the dummy, the declarer and himself. As he can see his and the dummy's hands, he knows how many the declarer holds. For example, look at Figure 164. West leads the 6. Six from eleven is five. East can see that he and the dummy hold four cards above the 6 between them, so South holds only one. He knows, incidentally, that South holds no more than three cards in the suit. Provided East beats as cheaply as possible whatever card North plays (by beating Jack with King or 7 with 9), then the

during the course of the auction, it is likely that he has a better suit than your best suit, and if you think this is so you should lead his suit. The general rule is to lead your highest card of his suit, unless you hold four cards in the suit or three cards headed by an honour, when you should lead your lowest. The value of holding back your honour in this case is shown by Figure 163. The lead of the 3 will allow East to make his Ace and then lead through South's K and J towards West's Queen, restricting South to one trick in the suit. The lead of the Queen would have allowed South to make King and Jack.

If you are on lead against a no-trump contract, and your side has not bid and your hand is nondescript, then your best lead is the fourth-highest card of your longest suit. This not only

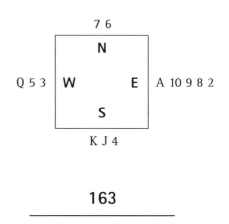

7 6

Q 5 3   W | N / E   A 10 9 8 2

S

K J 4

163

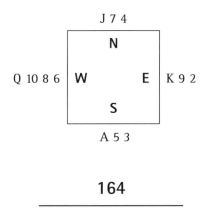

J 7 4

Q 10 8 6   W   E   K 9 2

A 5 3

164

declarer will make no more than one trick in the suit.

(b) The opening lead against a suit contract   Against a suit contract the demands are different. The attempt to establish a long suit is pointless, as instead of lower cards becoming winners they will be trumped. However, in some circumstances the lead of a long suit could be advantageous. For an example see Figure 165. This provides a good example of the difference between leading against no-trump and a suit contracts. Against a suit contract it would be pointless for West to lead his fourth-highest card: the declarer would make an easy trick with his Queen. However, if declarer leads Ace, he will win the first trick, retain the master card in the suit (King), and furthermore be

able to view dummy before he needs to lead to the second trick.

At the risk of getting ahead of ourselves, there is now a signal that East can use to encourage his partner to continue. It is called a high–low play, or *peter*. East, knowing that his partner has possibly led Ace from Ace and King (the higher of touching honours), will play the 9 before the 5. He will play the 5 on the next round, thus 'completing the peter'. This will tell partner that he is now out of the suit and needs to trump, or less often that he now holds the master card in the suit. In either case it is an invitation for his partner to lead the suit again. So West, on lead against a suit contract in Figure 165, will lead Ace, and East will play 9. Winning the trick, West will play King, winning the trick again and noticing his partner's 5.

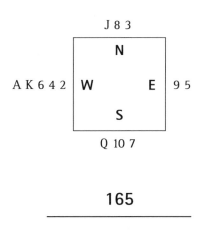

J 8 3

A K 6 4 2   W   E   9 5

Q 10 7

165

West will now lead 2, East will trump and the defenders will have the first three tricks in the bag.

Another safe lead against a suit contract is an honour from the top of a sequence, preferably a short and strong one like K, Q, J or Q, J, 10. This is likely to give nothing away.

A lead of a singleton or doubleton can be good if nothing else suggests itself. The idea is that on the second or third round, respectively, you will be able to ruff. It is of course a pointless lead if you have no trumps.

Similarly, if you hold, for instance, three small trumps but with a balanced hand and little prospect of being able to ruff, you might lead trumps. This can embarrass the declarer if the dummy is revealed with only two or three trumps and the declarer is hoping to use them to establish a side suit.

There is a case where a lead from a long suit is your best option. This is when you hold trumps yourself and can use a long side-suit of your own to force the declarer to use his own trumps. An example hand is shown in Figure 166. South is the declarer in 4 ♥. West leads the ♣ A, on which East plays an encouraging 9. West continues with ♣ J, which South ruffs. Whatever South does then (he might lay down Ace of trumps, then cross to the ♠ A to finesse in trumps, or he may cross to the ♠ A first to finesse twice in trumps), West will eventually regain

the lead (with a trump or ♦ K) and lead clubs again, forcing South to ruff again and reducing his trumps until South loses control of the trump suit and fails in his contract.

Card signalling

We have dealt already with the peter, or high–low signal. Look again at Figure 165. How does West know, when East

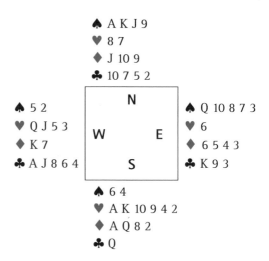

166

Against 4 ♥ played by South, repeated leading of clubs by West could weaken South's trumps sufficiently to beat the contract.

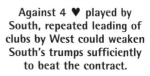

follows the lead of the Ace with the 9, that the 9 is the start of a peter? At first, he will suspect it might be, because 9 is a high card to play on the first round of a suit. When South follows with 7, West will be more sure that East is petering, because he can see in his own and dummy's hand the 8, 6, 4, 3 and 2, and if South's 7 is the lowest card he holds, East must have the 5. When East plays 5 under West's King on the second round, West knows that East is now either void or must be holding the master Queen.

When leading Ace from Ace and King, you need to try to work out if your partner's card is high or low. Without a doubleton or the Queen, your partner will play his lowest card, which is discouraging. In Figures 167 and 168 you are West, on lead. In Figure 167, East plays 3 on your lead of Ace and South follows with 6. Where is the 2? Unless South is bluffing, East holds 2 and is encouraging you to continue with a view to making his Queen on the third round. In Figure 168, on the other hand, East follows your Ace and North's 2 with 7, and South plays the 5. You can now see that the cards played, with those remaining in your hand and the dummy, account for the 2, 3, 4, 5 and 6. East's 7 was his lowest card. You should not therefore lead the King on the second round. As you can see, to do so would set up tricks for South's Queen and Jack once trumps had been drawn.

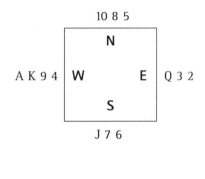

167

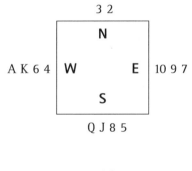

168

♠
♥
♦
♣

Another way of signalling comes when you must discard. There are complex signals to be made with discards, but the first and simplest rule to follow is that on your first discard, discard the suit you least want your partner to lead. In Figure 169, South is in a contract of 4 ♥. West leads ♣ 3 and South takes the first trick in dummy with ♣ 10. Mistakenly, South reasons, 'I can make three tricks in clubs and three in spades, and when the Ace of trumps is forced out, four in trumps to complete the contract. I must draw trumps first to ensure that none of my spades or clubs tricks is trumped.' So South leads Jack and 10 of trumps from dummy, which win as West ducks each time. On the second round East must discard. East would like diamonds to be led, so signals by discarding ♠ 6, not being interested in a spade lead. The declarer leads another trump, taken by West's Ace. West can see that continuing clubs is unlikely to succeed. As East doesn't want spades led, he leads a low diamond. East makes three diamond tricks and the contract is defeated.

Of course, South played poorly. Can you see how he should have made the contract? Having won the opening lead with ♣ 10, South should have spotted that his only threat was the loss of three diamond tricks plus the Ace of trumps. He should have immediately cashed ♣ K, returned to hand with ♠ K, and led ♣ A, discarding ♦ 7 from the

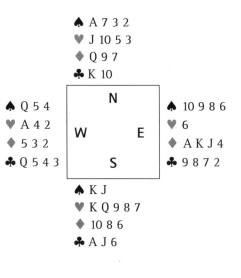

169

South is declarer in 4 ♥ and decides to draw trumps. By signalling with his discard on the second round, East encourages partner to lead a diamond and defeat the contract.

dummy. This reduces his diamond losers to two, as he can now trump in dummy a third round of the suit.

Second player low, third player high
Before bingo, people gathered together to play whist in whist drives. It was a principle of faith that 'second player plays low, third player plays high'. It is

♠
♥
♦
♣

The play

not a bad principle provided it is not regarded as an unbreakable rule. So long as you appreciate the basis for it, you can break it whenever you see a reason to do so. Consider West's hand in Figure 170. South, who is the declarer and needs to make a trick in the suit, leads 2. West, as second player, plays low. Playing the Queen would be pointless. North would beat it with King. If East holds the Ace (as he does), he will win the trick, but he would have done anyway, and West has wasted his Queen. If East doesn't hold the Ace, West has still wasted his Queen under North's King. West must assume that if 8 is played from the dummy, West can beat it without having to use the Ace. Notice that if West does play the Queen, beaten by both King and Ace, South will make a trick in the suit with his Jack. By withholding the Queen, West makes it impossible for South to make a trick in the suit (barring East mistakenly taking Ace and leading 5, with South playing 7).

Figure 171 shows an occasion when West, as the second player, is rightly justified in ignoring the principle and playing high. If South, as declarer, leads 7, West should play the King and take the trick. This could lose a trick if his partner, East, holds the bare Ace. On the other hand, should West play low and North win, West's now bare King could fall below the Ace on the next round, thus losing a trick. Better, therefore, for West to make sure of the trick and lead

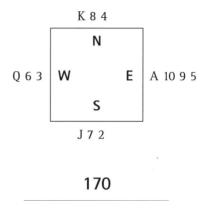

170

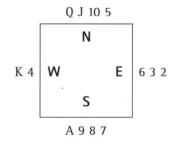

171

♠
♥
♦
♣

a suit which is more advantageous to his side.

The need for the third hand to play high is to prevent the opponents winning an easy trick with a low card. Figure 172 demonstrates the principle. West leads 5 (fourth-highest) against South's contract of 3NT. East must play the King. If South wins with the Ace, the defence will nevertheless win four tricks in the suit if they can regain the lead. If East plays 9, South wins with 10 and retains the Ace for another trick.

An instance when third player should *not* play high occurs in Figure 173. South is again declarer in 3NT and West leads the 5, on which North plays 2. East can see (by the Rule of Eleven) that South has only one card higher than 5. It could be Ace, King, 10 or 7. It is most likely to be Ace or King (otherwise South is unlikely to be in a no-trump contract, and anyway West might have led Ace if holding both Ace and King). If East plays the 9, retaining the Queen over dummy's Jack, forcing the declarer, if he wants, to win with Ace or King, he will restrict the declarer to one trick in the suit. If he plays Queen, declarer will later win a second trick with Jack as well. Playing 9 can only cost East a trick if declarer's highest card is 10 — and the defence can still take three tricks in the suit when back on lead.

On the whole, however, 'third player plays high' is usually the safest policy.

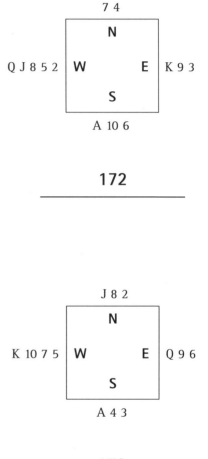

172

173

Leading through strength

If you are on lead and there are no obvious leads, it is best to lead through strength, setting the declarer a puzzle as to which card to play. In Figure 174 West is to lead against a contract by South. Little can be lost by leading a club through the dummy's Ace, Queen. If the declarer does not hold King, he is forced to play Ace, thus establishing East's King, or to hope that West has led away from the King, in which case he will play Queen and lose to East's King. As the cards lie, it forces the declarer to make a choice perhaps before he was ready to. Of course, if the declarer happens to hold the King, nothing is lost as little could prevent him making Ace, King and Queen anyway.

Leading up to weakness

This is the same principle as leading through strength. If East is on lead against South's contract in Figure 175, the lead of ♣ 10 towards dummy's weak holding is likely to force declarer into making a choice. As the cards lie, declarer cannot duck without the ♣ 10 winning the trick, in which case East will follow by leading ♣ 9. South has to choose between ♣ K or ♣ J, and whichever he plays is unlikely to make a trick in the suit.

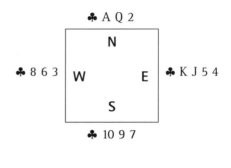

174

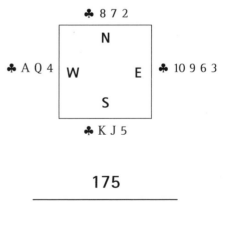

175

Covering an honour with an honour

This is another maxim from whist drives. It is a good principle but should not be followed blindly as there are occasions when it will not pay. The idea is best shown by the example of Figure 176. Against a 3NT contract by South, West leads ♣ J, and North plays ♣ Q. East must cover North's honour by beating it with another, his ♣ K. No matter that South wins with ♣ A, West's ♣ 10 is promoted to master, and South will win no more tricks in the suit. Had East allowed North's ♣ Q to win, South would have won a second trick with ♣ A.

However, Figure 177 shows an example where it would be wrong to cover an honour with an honour. South, the declarer, leads ♣ Q from dummy. If East plays ♣ K, South will win with ♣ A. South is now in a position to take a chance and lead towards the dummy's ♣ J and 9, finessing against the ♣ 10. This will succeed and the declarer could make four tricks in the suit. However, if East holds up his ♣ K and plays it on the second round when the declarer leads ♣ J from the dummy, the declarer will still win with ♣ A, but West's ♣ 10 will now be promoted to master card in the suit. Note that if East holds up his ♣ K on the first round and it transpires that West holds ♣ A, there is nothing lost – East/West will take at least two tricks in the suit.

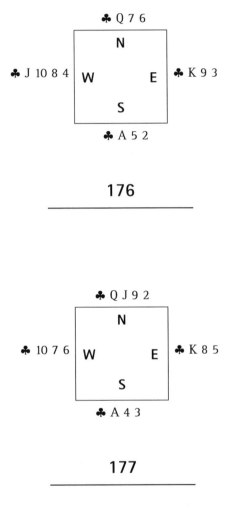

```
          ♣ Q 7 6
        ┌─────────┐
        │    N    │
♣ J 10 8 4 │ W     E │ ♣ K 9 3
        │    S    │
        └─────────┘
          ♣ A 5 2

            176
```

```
         ♣ Q J 9 2
        ┌─────────┐
        │    N    │
♣ 10 7 6 │ W     E │ ♣ K 8 5
        │    S    │
        └─────────┘
          ♣ A 4 3

            177
```

SUMMARY 4

SUMMARY

Summary

I hope you got this far. I hope you managed to find others to learn with, and that you started playing as soon as you'd read Getting to know Bridge. That would have made the other two parts easier to assimilate, particularly the complicated business of bidding. There will no doubt be many details you cannot remember, but that will not stop you getting great pleasure from playing and you will remember more and more as you play more. Remember that the bidding system advocated is only a recommendation, and only one of thousands invented and used over the years. If a new partner asks about your system do not be dismayed. He only wants to agree with you that you open 1NT with 16–18 points, that if you open 2 ♣ it means you have around 23 points, and so on. Most players will use the same basic system as you, but if you and a new partner differ on a particular point you can agree whose system you follow. Read and enjoy Bridge columns in newspapers and magazines, but do not expect immediately to understand everything you read. There are whole books written about Bridge techniques which could almost be said to start where this one finishes. You will often find terms not used in this book. But no matter — there is always something that rubs off, and you will be improving your knowledge painlessly while you read.

Bridge columnists often write of duplicate Bridge, which is a competitive form of Bridge where the hands are pre-arranged. There are two pairs in each team. In one room the pair from Team A play the North/South cards while Team B plays East/West. Concurrently, in the other room, the other pair from Team B plays the same North/South cards while the other Team A pair play East/West. Chance, in theory at least, is eliminated since both teams are playing the same cards against each other. The scores from the two rooms are added, and the team with more points scores according to the discrepancy — the difference in the two scores is converted into what are called International Match Points. The winning team is that ahead at the end of, say, 64 boards, a board being the name given to a deal. This is ideal for Bridge writers, because they can compare how experts played the same hands in two rooms, and can discuss where, perhaps, one pair went wrong while another got it right. Of course, it makes for entertaining and instructive reading.

Bridge has its etiquette. Only the declarer has the right to touch the dummy, so do not touch it, even if it was your own hand, nor the tricks already won on the table. Do not discuss the play as it is progressing, or indeed make any comment touching on the play. After the hand, and especially when learning with friends, ask for comments on your hand if you wish, but do not criticize somebody else's play if not asked to. And above all, do not criticize your partner. Apart from anything else, an unhappy or upset partner is not going to play so well on the next deal. Remember, it is only a card game, even if it might be the world's best.

Continue to play, continue to learn and, above all, continue to enjoy it.

QUICK REFERENCE
SCORING TABLE

• •

When an undoubled contract is made:

Score below the line at the following rate:

When spades or hearts are trumps,	30	points per trick over six
When diamonds or clubs are trumps,	20	per trick over six
When the contract is in no-trumps,	40	for the first trick over six,
	30	per trick thereafter

Overtricks are entered above the line at the same rate. A score of 100 points below the line wins a game and a line is drawn beneath it. There is no bonus for winning a game, except in an unfinished rubber (see below).

When a doubled or redoubled contract is made:

The trick score is multiplied by two when a doubled contract has been made, by four when it has been redoubled. There is an additional bonus of 50 points, scored above the line, for any doubled contract that is made, and 100 points for any redoubled contract that is made.

Overtricks, scored above the line, are scored as follows:

Not vulnerable 100 per trick when doubled, 200 when redoubled

Vulnerable 200 per trick doubled, 400 when redoubled

Penalties when a contract is defeated:

Not vulnerable

Undoubled:	50 per undertrick
Doubled:	100 for the first undertrick, 200 for each undertrick thereafter
Redoubled:	200 for the first undertrick, 400 for each undertrick thereafter

Vulnerable

Undoubled:	100 per undertrick
Doubled:	200 for the first undertrick, 300 for each undertrick thereafter
Redoubled:	400 for the first undertrick, 600 for each undertrick thereafter

Bonus for honours:

For four of the five trump honours (A, K, Q, J and 10) in one hand: 100
For all five trump honours (A, K, Q, J and 10) in one hand: 150
For four Aces in a no-trump contract in one hand: 150

Bonus for slam:

Not vulnerable small slam 500, grand slam 1,000
Vulnerable small slam 750, grand slam 1,500

Bonus for rubber:

For winning a rubber two games to nil: 700
For winning a rubber two games to one: 500

Bonus in unfinished rubber:

For having won a game: 300
For having a part-score in an unfinished game: 50

♠
♥
♦
♣

GLOSSARY OF BRIDGE TERMS

· ·

Above the line

Where scores, except those for tricks bid and made, are entered on the score sheet.

Auction

The bidding or period of bidding.

Balanced hand

A hand in which the suits are more or less evenly distributed, such as 4–3–3–3.

Below the line

Where scores for tricks bid and made are entered on the score sheet.

Bid

A call with which a player undertakes to win a certain number of tricks in a specified trump suit or without trumps.

Blackwood

A bidding convention used to determine how many Aces partner has (see page 111).

Board

In Duplicate Bridge, a hand, e.g. a match of 64 boards.

Call

Any bid, double, redouble or pass made during the auction.

Contract

The final bid of the auction, which announces the declarer's undertaking to make a certain number of tricks with or without a specified trump suit.

Conventional bid

A bid with a special meaning.

Crossruff

A means of attempting to make a contract by trumping suits in hand and dummy.

Cue bid

A bid to indicate to partner control of the suit bid.

Declarer

The player who first mentions the suit of the final contract and who plays the hand, including that of dummy.

Defender

In bidding, a player whose opponents have opened the bidding; in play, an opponent of the declarer.

Denomination

The trump suit (or no-trumps) in which the contract is to be played.

Discard

A card played which is not of the suit led or a trump; to play such a card.

Distribution

The shape of a player's hand in terms of the number of cards in each suit.

Double

A call that increases the penalty for a contract that is not made, or increases the value of a contract that is made.

Doubleton

A holding of two cards in a suit.

Duck

To decline to take a trick by playing a low card.

Dummy

The hand of the declarer's partner, which is exposed on the table after the opening lead.

Finesse

A means of winning a trick with a card that is not the highest available.

Fit

A hand that fits well with the hand held by the player's partner.

Follow suit

To play a card of the suit led.

Forcing bid

A bid that requires partner to continue bidding.

Game

A score of 100 or more below the line, which wins one phase of Bridge.

Game contract

A contract that, if made, will win a game.

Grand slam

A contract to make, or the making, of all 13 tricks in a deal.

Guard

A holding in a suit, e.g. Ace or King, Queen, which prevents opponents from winning a string of tricks in that suit.

Hold-up

The holding back of a winning card for later use.

Honour, honour cards

The Ace, King, Queen, Jack or 10.

Intermediates

Valuable cards below the top honours, e.g. 10, 9 and 8.

Jump raise

A bid higher than necessary, used to show strength.

Lead

The first card played to a trick.

Limit bid

A bid that conveys limited strength to partner.

Major suit

Spades or hearts.

Minor suit

Diamonds or clubs.

Open

To make the first bid.

Opening lead

The first lead of a deal.

Overbid

To bid higher than the previous bid.

♠
♥
♦
♣

Overcall

A defender's bid higher than an opponent's opening bid.

Overruff

To play a trump higher than an opponent's trump.

Overtricks

Tricks made in excess of the contract.

Overtrump

See Overruff.

Part-score

A score from a contract which is less than the 100 points required for game.

Pass

A call meaning a player does not wish to bid, double or redouble.

Penalty

Points awarded to the other side for failing to make a contract.

Penalty double

A double intended to inflict a penalty on the declarer, rather than one intended for take-out (q.v.).

Penalty pass

A pass made when your partner has doubled, intending you to bid (see Take-out double). By passing you convert the double to one intended to inflict penalties.

Peter

An encouraging signal to partner by playing a card higher than the lowest held.

Point count

A system of assessing a hand's strength by awarding points to certain high-value cards.

Pre-emptive bid

A high bid made with a weak hand with the purpose of crabbing opponents' bidding space.

Promote

To promote low cards in a suit to master cards by leading the suit and clearing out the higher cards, sometimes at the expense of conceding tricks.

Raise

To raise the level of the bid, e.g. to raise 3 ♥ to 4 ♥.

Rebid

Opener's second bid after partner's response.

Redouble

A call that increases penalties or bonuses further after a bid has been doubled.

Response

A bid made in reply to partner's opening bid.

Rubber

A set of two or three games. Whichever side wins two games wins the rubber.

Ruff

To play a trump.

Sacrifice

A bid to win a contract that bidder is not hopeful of making – it is intended to save points by stopping opponents making a bigger score.

Sequence

A run of adjacent cards in a suit.

Shift

See Switch.

Side suit

A suit other than the trump suit.

Sign-off

A bid intended to convey to partner to stop bidding further.

Singleton

A holding of one card in a suit.

Slam

A contract to make 12 tricks (small slam) or 13 tricks (grand slam), or the making of them.

Small slam

A contract to make 12 tricks, or the making of them.

Stayman

A bidding convention that asks partner to name a major suit in which he holds four cards (see page 98).

Stopper

See Guard.

Switch

In bidding, to bid a new suit, e.g. to switch from diamonds to spades. Also called Shift.

System

A method of bidding agreed between two partners.

Take-out double

A double intended to convey a signal to partner, who is to 'take out' the double by bidding again.

Tenace

A holding, such as Ace and Queen, which guarantees two tricks if the holder is the last player in the trick.

Trap pass

A pass with a strong hand, intended to trap opponents into rash bidding.

Trick

A set of four cards, one played by each player.

Tricks on top

The tricks which can be made from holding the master cards, e.g. the Aces, and the Kings when the Aces are also held.

Trump

A suit named in the contract that beats a card led in a side suit; a card of that suit, and the act of playing it. See also Ruff.

Undertricks

The number of tricks by which a declarer fails to make his contract.

Void

A holding of no cards in a suit.

Vulnerable

The state of a side that has won a game, and thus face higher penalties or bonuses in scoring.

INDEX

● ● ● ● ● ● ● ● ● ● ● ● ● ● ● ● ● ● ●

Index

♠
♥
♦
♣

Index

Index and Acknowledgements

Acknowledgements

Executive Editor: Trevor Davies
Editor: Jessica Cowie
Executive Art Editor: Peter Burt
Design: Publish on Demand Ltd.
Illustrations: Publish on Demand Ltd., and Line + Line
Senior Production Controller: Ian Paton